THE IMPLICATIONS

The importance of unity
in a fractured world

MALCOLM DUNCAN

MONARCH
BOOKS

Published by Monarch Books (an imprint of Lion Hudson plc)

Wilkinson House, Jordan Hill Road, Oxford OX2 8DR, England

Email: monarch@lionhudson.com www.lionhudson.com/monarch

and by Essential Christian, 14 Horsted Square, Uckfield, East Sussex TN22 1QG

Tel: 01825 746530 Email: info@essentialchristian.org

Web: www.essentialchristian.com

ISBN 978 0 85721 884 1

e-ISBN 978 0 85721 885 8

First edition 2017

Acknowledgments

Scripture quotations are from The New Revised Standard Version of the Bible copyright © 1989 by the Division of Christian Education of the National Council of Churches in the USA. Used by permission. All Rights Reserved.

p. 119–20: Extract from *Our Life Together: A Memoir in Letters* © 2008 Jean Vanier, reprinted by permission of Darton, Longman and Todd

A catalogue record for this book is available from the British Library

Printed and bound in the UK, July 2017, LH26

One for All has captured what is for me a central theme of scripture and a key prophetic challenge that God wants to bring to the Church at this time: in the midst of amazing diversity as God's people, God has called us to recognise and celebrate our unity – being members of the same family, brothers and sisters in Christ. This is a unity which brings smiles in heaven and greater effectiveness on earth.

Steve Clifford, General Director, Evangelical Alliance

Malcolm's wonderful book serves the body of Christ in a time of tensions and divisions by reminding us that we are, and could only ever be, one body.

Paul Harcourt, National Leader of New Wine England

The unity of the church is central to Christ's prayers for his people but is sadly so often missing from our priorities. In this timely book Malcolm Duncan shows us not just why unity matters to God but also how it can become a reality for us. He refuses to give pat answers or to back away from the real issues we face. You may not agree with all of his conclusions but you will be challenged by the grace of his approach and the courage of his convictions.

Dr Krish Kandiah, Founding director of Home for Good and author of *God is Stranger*

One For All is an extraordinary book, a useful manual, a personal challenge and an absolute must-read for us all as we share faith, hope and love in a fractured world.

Cathy Madavan, writer, speaker, member of Spring Harvest planning group and author of *Digging for Diamonds*

National church leader and prophet Malcolm Duncan offers us the glorious vision of a united Church – one which fulfils Jesus' high priestly prayer, which receives the Father's commanded blessing, which confirms the Spirit's baptism into one body, and which causes the world to sit up and take note.

Simon Ponsonby, Pastor of Theology at St Aldates, Oxford

Also by Malcolm Duncan:

Kingdom Come: The Local Church as a Catalyst for Change

Risk Takers: The Life God Intends for You

40 Days with Jesus: An Invitation to Know Him Better

I Want to be a God Gazer: Yearning for Intimacy with the Saviour

Unbelievable: Confident Faith in a Skeptical World

Spring Harvest 2014 Theme Guide: Your Daily Guide to Exploring Unbelievable

Fleeting Shadows: How Christ Transforms the Darkness

Building a Better World: Faith at Work for Change in Society

One for All: The Foundations

This book is dedicated to the following people:

Debbie Duncan – I thank God for you.

Ellie Knight – welcome to our family – and our son Benjamin. May your marriage be rich, deep and Christ-centred.

The Staff Team at Gold Hill – thank you for your passion for extending the kingdom of God and being willing to sacrifice so much for His glory. May you always keep Him at the centre of your service.

To all those Christian leaders who refuse to give up on the idea that we are stronger together than we are apart. Thank you for your persistence and your vision. Keep going.

Contents

Acknowledgments

I could not write without the ongoing grace and mercy of Almighty God. My first and deepest thanks go to Him.

I am grateful, once again, to my family for their prayers and encouragement. My wife Debbie and my children – Matthew, Benjamin, Anna, and Riodhna – are a wonderful blessing.

I am grateful to my church family at Gold Hill and to the wider network of Christians who pray for and support my ministry – thank you so much for your ongoing prayers and love. I also want to thank the elders, staff, and church council at Gold Hill for their encouragement and support.

I am indebted to my colleagues at Spring Harvest for their support and encouragement, and their patience, in the preparation and delivery of this material and the first book – thank you. Particular thanks go to Peter Martin, who is both a colleague in ministry and a dear friend, and to his wife, Karen.

Thank you also to the team at Monarch and at Lion. In the midst of great change and uncertainty you have been a huge support. Thank you to Simon Cox – all the best for the future – and to Jenny and Suzanne for your help, encouragement, and support.

Lastly, I want to express a huge and heartfelt thank you to all the Spring Harvest family. It has been a joy to lead you for the past five years and I look forward to continuing to play my part in the leadership team. You haven't managed to get rid of me yet. You, the Spring Harvest guests, are like an extended family, and I thank God for all you do and all you are. Never give up on God's dream.

Soli Deo Gloria

Malcolm Duncan
Buckinghamshire
May 2017

Crossing Barriers

Once we understand that unity is essential we also need to know how to do it. Going from grasping a truth to actually living it is something we humans often find difficult. We can give mental assent to an idea, but making that idea a reality within our lives is much more challenging.[1]

Unity matters to God and it matters to us. The way we grapple with our differences has more influence in our lives than we could possibly imagine. Finding ways of sharing life and mission together in the Christian church has always been important, but it might be true to say that it has never been as important as it is today. When disintegration and tribalism are on the increase in the society of which the church is a part, the church is called to be an example of unity, of love, and of hope. If the church of Jesus Christ cannot celebrate, protect, and invest in the unities of identity, purpose, mission, and worship that God has given us, then the societies of which we are part will not only continue to disintegrate but will also experience that disintegration at an increasing rate. The world needs the church to be united, but not at the expense of Truth. Our society does not need a church that is united at the point of lowest common agreement, but rather it needs to see a church that can be robust in its conversations, true to its principles, and aware of the challenges of working alongside one another, but fundamentally committed to finding every possible way of sticking together. It might not always be possible, but it should always be the default to which we are set. God wants His church to be one. Our society needs the church to demonstrate this reality, yet it can be exceptionally difficult for this to happen. Unity isn't a dirty word; it is a high calling.

Society in the first quarter of the twenty-first century and the two or three generations that follow it has the potential to become so deeply fractured that it will take centuries to sort out the mess that such divisions will leave behind. On the surface of our life together, six things threaten our society's safety: a growing gap between the rich and the poor, rising political instability, social uncertainty, economic fragility, family disintegration, and spiritual confusion. These six issues affect us wherever we are. In the British Isles their impacts are felt from the Shetland Islands, nestled in the cold, raging seas of the North Atlantic, to the Channel Islands, sheltered in the busy waters of the English Channel; from Tearaght Island, sitting 12.5 kilometres west of the Dingle Peninsula in the glistening waters of the Western Atlantic, to Ness Point near Lowestoft in Suffolk.

These challenges are not localized to the British Isles. These same six issues raise their heads in the United States, from Hawaii to New England and from Minnesota to Texas. They are seen across continental Europe and across the mountains, plains, and deserts of Africa. Egypt is struggling with potential disintegration, as is South Africa. It doesn't matter where you look, because the issues are found everywhere. Australia and New Zealand and the nations of Australasia face similar uncertainties to the rest of the world, as does the vast continent of Asia.

Of course, there are arguments in geopolitics about what has caused these challenges, and concerning how to address them. Is the gap between the rich and the poor caused by unfair systems of taxation and a lack of intervention from government? If you believe this to be the case, then you are likely to be on the left of the political spectrum. Or is it caused by too much intervention by government and a lack of social mobility, entrepreneurial investment, and inspiring people to lift themselves out of poverty? If you believe it is the latter, then you are more likely to be on the right of the political spectrum.

Is political instability being caused by weak governments who are afraid to stand up for their people, or is it being caused by a growing sense of insularity and nationalism?

Is social uncertainty a result of the global phenomenon of mass migration and the cultural changes it brings, or is it being caused by a loss of national identities in the maelstrom of modern-day ideas and liberalization?

And what about our economic fragility? Did bad banking in the first decade of the twenty-first century cause that, or was it the result of personal greed, overspending, and unwise fiscal choices by countries like Greece, Spain, and the United States?

Is family disintegration a result of society's failure to adapt to new ideas of what it means to be a family, or is it the result of a loss of commitment to the family altogether?

And what of spiritual confusion – is this caused by myriad choices of spirituality that now confront people, or is it caused by a loss of confidence in the core tenets of some of the world's faiths? Is radical Islam to blame for the crisis of spirituality? Perhaps it is bland and diluted Christianity? Or is it that people don't know what they believe any more?

Life together – the bigger issue

Behind the great challenges of the six issues, however, there is a deeper challenge. We are fracturing. Our communities are becoming more and more prone to division. Driven by fear, shaped by apprehension about "others", and fashioned by a rhetoric of self-defensiveness, we seem to lack politicians who can paint a picture of what a healthy, whole, and united society or community can look like. We are losing one another. Whether it is expressed through the election of Donald Trump, the UK decision to exit the European Union, the French election of President Emmanuel Macron, or the Scottish and Irish arguments of independence and separation, our societies are looking away from those that are different from ourselves and are seeking solace, security, and stability in a new isolationism. For some, this brings safety; for others, it brings a loss of opportunity. We are moving away from ideas of a bigger unity to definitions of community that are smaller, narrower, and easier to define – and perhaps to police.

This is where the possibility of the mission and the witness of the Christian church steps in. We need to find a new, better way of doing life together. What if we, the followers of Jesus Christ, were able to demonstrate what a healthy unity can look like? What if we, the Christian church, could demonstrate to a fracturing world that we do not have to fracture to be safe? What if our commitment to love one another, stand together, and serve together could be a powerful witness to a disintegrating world that community is better than isolation? What if local congregations of ordinary people could show those around them that there is a way for people from different social, ethnic, and political backgrounds to live together? What if the unity of the church could be one of the greatest witnesses of God's love and grace to the world that is breaking apart around us? What if those desperate to be part of a family could see that family in the church? What if the church were to demonstrate to the nation around us what it means to stick together? What if the next few generations of our society could see a church united in our mission, our calling, and our loyalties? And, as the old political boundaries of left and right give way to new boundaries that are yet to be fully defined but include liberty, community values, and nationhood, what if the church could provide a model of being community that could inspire new conversations, new ideas, and new aspirations?

Beyond idealism

The idea of Christian community and unity that can be a witness to the world could easily appear to be idealistic and naïve. You might look at the divisions within the church and then question, with wide-eyed wonder, how I could possibly argue that the unity of the church could be a gift to the societies that surround us. "Look at the way we are treating one another," you might suggest incredulously. "We fall out over issues that are secondary; we separate from one another rather than work things out; we are communities of suspicion, competition, and isolation." You might even add, "We don't tolerate difference; we reject those who do not accept our cultures; we force people to conform to our patterns of behaviour and lifestyle! How could we possibly be a force for good, and an example of unity and common purpose that could inspire others?"

While I do not deny that many of these arguments are true, I do not think we need to accept that this is the way is has to *stay*. My argument is that the unity of the church is a by-product of something else – a new and revitalized commitment to a higher goal and a greater common aim. That higher goal is the reality of who God is in the form of the Father, the Son, and the Holy Spirit, and the greater common aim is the proclamation of the gospel to the world, and our partnership, as followers of Jesus Christ, with the mission of God in the world. It is as we return to the truth of who God is and what God wants us *to be* and *to do* in the world that we can demonstrate a powerful unity to the communities around us. It is as we discover the unity that God has given us and we walk in it together that the world around us will see that there is hope for a greater common good. Our witness to the world may well begin with a better measure of humility and honesty about our own weaknesses and failings. I believe that if we were to allow our love for God and our love for one another to be of paramount importance, then our witness of unity to the world would be transformative. I want to suggest that our goal should not be unity, but rather love that is rooted deeply in the truth of who God is and in His mission for the world. In the words of the German pastor and theologian, Dietrich Bonhoeffer:

> *The person who loves their dream of community will destroy community, but the person who loves those around them will create community.*[2]

Jesus Christ made it quite plain to His disciples that they were to love God with all their hearts, minds, souls, and strength and that they were to love their neighbours as they loved themselves.[3] Followers of Jesus are also commanded to love one another,[4] and to love our enemies.[5] Christian community is grounded in these realities. No one is excluded from these definitions. If we were to categorize every human being who has ever lived, they would fall into one of these definitions. Therefore the implications of this are very simple: there is no one whom we do not love as Christians. In *One for All: The Implications* I want to explore what an honest, robust Christian unity might look like and what its impact on the world around us might be. At no point am I arguing for a bland, truthless, lifeless ecumenism that makes unity the aim of the enterprise. Instead, I am arguing for a unity that puts the truth of who God is, what He has done, and what He has called us to *do* and to *be* at the centre of our efforts. It is as we do this that we will be able to demonstrate a unity that is beyond naïvety to the world around us.

The unity that I am arguing for and want to encourage you to commit to is not easy. It demands a willingness to embrace humility insofar as we must recognize the limits of our own understanding. It also demands a willingness to wrestle with the truth, to think through what we believe and why we believe it, and a relentless commitment to the gospel of the Lord Jesus Christ, as well as a wholehearted pursuit of God's mission to the world. That means that sometimes we will not be able to agree. We may even have to separate, but even in those situations we can find a way of pointing back to Christ – at least that is what I will argue.

This robust, strong, intentional unity also involves a willingness to listen to others and to be willing to hear them properly. Bill Clinton, the former President of the United States of America, speaking at the funeral of the Irish Republican leader, Martin McGuinness, spoke of one of the key ways in which unity and peace could be protected. Clinton reminded those who were listening that if peace were to be maintained and unity were to be strengthened, then those who have legitimate grievances on both sides of an argument must be willing to embrace the future together. He went on to comment on a conversation that he had once had with Nelson Mandela, who was receiving criticism for his efforts to bring a new peace and unity to South Africa. Mandela was being attacked by those on his own side, who felt he was going too far to protect unity and peace. When Clinton asked what Mandela was saying in defence of his continued efforts at peace, Mandela replied:

> *They think I have sold them out… but I tell them that I spent twenty-seven years in jail; and they took all my best years away; and I didn't see my children grow up; and it ruined my marriage; and a lot of my friends were killed; and if I can get over it you can too. We gotta build the future.*[6]

Clinton suggested that peace and unity was not an "event" but a process to which each generation must commit itself. He argued that if we are to build peace and unity then we must allow our definition of "them" to decrease and our definition of "us" to increase. Commenting on McGuinness's life, Clinton said, "He expanded the definition of us and shrunk the definition of them."[7]

Therein lies one of the great challenges for us if we are to take unity seriously. We must allow ourselves to be willing to increase the definition of "us". This is not easy. It demands a willingness to create the most minimum of essentials, and for that reason those minimum essentials must be of the highest quality and of the utmost importance.

My thoughts and reflections in *One for All: The Implications* are rooted in the conviction that our unity as fellow Christians must be rooted in the highest source, be built around the strongest commitments, be evidenced in the most intentional choices, and be expressed in the deepest ways. In *The Implications* I set out what I believe those things to be. The highest source of Christian unity lies in our common identity in Christ. The strongest commitments of our unity are twofold. Firstly, the commitment to preach the gospel of the Lord Jesus Christ – that He died for our sins, that He was buried, and that He was raised from the dead on the third day according to the Scriptures.[8] Secondly, to be committed to the mission and the work of God that He has called us to in making disciples and demonstrating His love, justice, compassion, and mercy to the world.

These two commitments of gospel proclamation and kingdom mission are not the same thing. Our mission flows from the gospel but the gospel does not flow from the mission. I argue that our most intentional choices are found in our commitments to love God together and to love one another. In these pages I begin to explore what it means to love one another and what it means to love God together.

One for All: The Foundations

There is so much to explore within the theme of Christian unity. It is for that reason I found it necessary to write two books on the subject. My first work, *One for All: The Foundations*, was published early in 2017 as the theological foundation for the Spring Harvest event of the same year. In it I outlined some of the key theological arguments for Christian unity from three sections of the Scripture. I explored the "High Priestly Prayer" of Jesus in John 17, the great declaration of unity expressed by the Apostle Paul at the beginning of Ephesians 4, and the promise of God's blessing on unity expressed by the psalmist in Psalm 133.[9] There is one section from *One for All: The Foundations* that I have chosen to reproduce in this volume. It is the chapter entitled "God's Plea".[10] It is my paraphrase of a number of key Scriptures surrounding unity and its importance to us, and I am convinced enough of their centrality to include it in this volume as well.

I set out the reasons for Spring Harvest exploring the theme of unity in 2017 in *One for All: The Foundations*,[11] as well as some of the challenges that the church faces when it comes to the reality of loving one another and loving the world. Spring Harvest is an evangelical festival that has been used as a catalyst for unity, mission, and mobilization for almost forty years. We believe that it is more important than ever that Christians across the United Kingdom and beyond are encouraged to hold on to the truths of the gospel, the call of God upon the evangelical church to be committed to conversion, the cross, the truth of the Bible, the unique character and work of the Lord Jesus Christ, and the importance of Christian activism in society.[12] In addition, we are convinced that Spring Harvest can reach out to other Christian festivals and movements both within and outwith the evangelical traditions of the church to build a stronger and more effective witness to the unity of the church. Many of those who attend Spring Harvest come from evangelical churches, but many others do not. As a festival, we celebrate who we are and the unique identity that it brings to us, and at the same time we want to find ways of celebrating our common life with the wider family of God. We do so, not because we are unclear about our identity and the beating heart of Spring Harvest, but because we are very clear – and that clarity leads to both a confidence in who God has called us to be and a humility that enables us to listen well and partner effectively with others within the Christian community.

One for All: The Implications has been written to give arms and legs to the theological convictions set out in the first book. In each chapter I want to suggest ways in which we might help one another into a deeper experience of the reality of Christian unity. In it I am seeking to be pastoral, practical, and purposeful about unity.

It is my prayer that *The Implications* will help readers to dig into the truths of the first book (and it is important to remember the theological and biblical convictions that hold us together) and to build strong, pragmatic principles in the ministries of their local churches and in the context of their local communities. The Spring Harvest event in 2017 explored the issues that are set out here in a series of seminars, lectures, discussions, debates, and celebrations. The recordings of those sessions, which may well help you to grapple with them more deeply, are available for download, and they bring together a series of speakers and resources from across the spectrum of the church.[13]

The church of Jesus Christ has a clear identity *in Christ*, we have a clear commission *from Christ*, and we have a clear destiny *with Christ*. One of the speakers at the 2017 Spring Harvest event, Sim Dendy,[14] challenged the guests to remember that purpose, with a declaration entitled "We Are Sent":[15]

WE
ARE
SENT.
For this time, this moment.

You being here is not some sort of accident,
Or just the luck of the draw.
You.

You are here for so much more than sacraments,
And self-righteous religiosity,
You are here because you're meant to be.
You're sent to be,
Hell bent to see,
People set free,
And made new.
You.

You are…
SENT to be grace in the face of hatred,
SENT to sow peace in war-torn land,
SENT to show joy to the despised and the hated.
SENT to light up dark places and
SENT to put a smile on sad faces.
SENT to the "Foodbank users" and the well fed,
SENT to the homeless sleeping on a cardboard bed,
SENT to patch up wounded lives,
SENT to care for abandoned wives,
SENT to lift the weight off the weighed-down shoulders of
*   PTSD-riddled soldiers.*
SENT to the orphans abandoned at birth,
SENT to the anorexic with AWOL self-worth,
SENT to the widow, to those still mourning,
SENT to the job-seekers where depression is dawning,
SENT to those stuck in the daily grind,
SENT to those who have given up any hope of finding
*   anything worth celebrating.*

SENT to the "haves",
SENT to the "have-nots".
SENT to the parents just about managing,
SENT to the rich young gap year travelling,
SENT to millennials and digital natives,
SENT to artists, musicians, creatives,
SENT to the young and the young at heart.
You've been SENT from your first breath and you'll be
SENT 'til your last.
SENT as ONE CHURCH on a MISSION, to ONE
WORLD for ONE PURPOSE,
On purpose,
By ONE GOD.
WE
ARE
SENT.

Reaching out and reaching up

The cross of Jesus Christ sits at the heart of the Christian faith as a symbol of hope. It reminds us that Christ died, was buried, and rose again. To followers of Christ it speaks of His sacrifice, His death, and His resurrection. Yet it also speaks of unity. It is embedded in the earth, deeply rooted in the realities of life on this planet. It also points upward, toward the God who sees us, knows us, and has intervened in human history. It points outward too – one arm of the cross toward a man who rejected who Christ was and the other to a man who accepted who Christ was.[16]

That simple picture of the cross reminds us of the call of God upon His people. We are rooted in the realities of our time. This means our cultures, our contexts, and our communities. Yet at the same time we point toward God, to the One who has intervened in time and space through His Son, our Saviour, the Lord Jesus Christ. As His people, we reach out our hands to one another – to those who have embraced Christ and experienced His forgiveness and His mercy, and to those who are yet to accept Him, who may even reject Him. We do all of this as His people united by what He has done for us and by who we are *in Him*.

I am a local church pastor. Our village, nestled on the outskirts of London, is home to a vibrant community of people from a range of different social, cultural, and spiritual backgrounds. Within fifteen minutes' drive from where I live are the multicultural centres of Uxbridge, High Wycombe, and Watford. Not only do these communities have high levels of diversity, they also have high levels of deprivation, social breakdown, and cultural crises. They are great places to live, but they are also volatile and challenging communities. In fact, in recent terrorist attacks or terror plots, a number of the people involved have come from some of the communities near where I live.

Our church family is good at global mission. We can reach out more easily to cultures and communities on the other side of the world than we can to the cultures and communities in our own vicinity. I believe it would be easier for me to persuade people to go and plant a church in Pakistan than it would be to see people volunteer to reach the Bengali communities in Slough or Uxbridge. Many in my village are uneasy about immigration; they are not certain about the best way to cope with the increasing numbers of people who want to come to the UK to find safety and a home.

Our church family is trying to work out how we can best serve those from different cultures, including those who are refugees, while at the same time helping our geographic community to let go of some of their fears and uncertainties – and it is really hard. We face questions ourselves; we are trying to find our way. We've made some good decisions and some bad ones. We're still not clear about what the best strategy is to bring about the changes we know God wants to see in our church and in our community. Many local pastors will feel exactly the same way.

In addition, our church family is committed to unity across the local church in our area – but we know there is more that we can do in this regard too. We already celebrate high levels of mutual support and input as local churches, but we know there is more to do. That can be hard too. Not everyone in our church family is happy about the alliances and the partnerships that we are committed to. At the same time, we are committed to learning how to do mission, to unity, and to loving one another better. We want to learn new ways, try new things, and see what works and what doesn't.

I am not the only local pastor or church leader who struggles to make the theology of unity and joint mission work on the ground. We need help to turn the convictions of our conscience into the principles of our practice. Borrowing an image from Tom Kraeuter will help us here: just like a child building a house made of Lego, we need to make sure that the fabrics of our unity are the principles and priorities that God has given to us.[17]

My prayer is that *One for All: The Implications* will be a book that helps all of us to do mission and unity more effectively. We need each other if we are to accomplish the great task to which God has called us.

Reflecting locally

For now, perhaps it behoves us to reflect on our own communities. Having begun this chapter by exploring the great geopolitical issues of our day, I invite you to consider now your own community.

Firstly, think about your community of faith itself. Local churches can be riven with divisions and factions. We argue and fight over the most mundane of things. Too quickly we allow our preferences to become our prejudices. Our pastors and our leaders need our prayers and our love more than they need our criticisms and our resentment. There is enough division in the world around us without those are part of a local church adding to it.

Perhaps you can take a few moments now to pray for your local church and for your local church leaders? Why not drop them a card expressing your gratitude to them, or pick up the phone and invite them for a coffee and thank them for their service to Christ? How can you be a source of unity, love, and affirmation in your local church? How can you set an example in word and deed to those around you? As you dream about what your local church could become, you might want to take a moment to become the change that you want to see in that worshipping community. Instead of waiting for someone else to make the first move, perhaps you can?

Secondly, think about the wider church in your local community. Are you united? So often, in our communities, our dictum is that we will do things on our own unless we have to do them with someone else. What if you were to turn that around and make it your purpose to support unity across the local church? What if you were to become a champion for the idea that there is only one church in your community and that your congregation is a part of it rather than the sum total of it? How might your church celebrate the wider church? How might you play your part? How might you see Christ in the lives of other local Christians?

What does it mean for all Christians to find their identity *in Him*? Let's see if we can find out in the chapter entitled "In Him", but first we turn our attention to what God might say to us through His word.

God's Plea

I cannot begin to express to you how important I think the issue of unity is for the church in the world today.[18] Without it we have little or nothing to say to the world around us. I cannot find the words that are necessary to articulate the cry of my heart for us to stand together. I am utterly convinced that when we stand together and serve together we are stronger together. Rather than try to find my own arguments, I want to present to you the pleas of some of the Bible's writers as they reflected on the importance of unity. I have drawn together some of the words prayed or spoken by Jesus and some of the words written by Paul, John, Matthew, Peter, and one of the psalmists, and I have crafted a plea for unity that I believe represents their heart and their yearning.

The letter that follows is not a word-for-word translation of their words but I do believe it resonates with their yearning for Christ's church to be one. The Scriptures I have interpreted are themselves inspired of God and so they echo God's own heart cry, articulated through the original authors of these words, for unity and togetherness. The issue of our relationship with one another is deeply important to God and should, therefore, be deeply important to us. It is the cry of my own heart to each of us that we might give ourselves to being one.

Each section of the letter is my own interpretative paraphrase of specific passages of Scripture that I have crafted together. The original excerpts are detailed in the endnotes. The original authors capture the yearning of God's heart that we might be one. May we hear that passion as we read these words, and may we reflect on what each of us can do to preserve and protect the unity of the body of Christ.

To every single brother and sister in Christ

I am pleading with you with all the passion, intensity, and authority that Jesus has given me and because we are each under His Lordship and therefore irrevocably connected to one another. I beg you to recognize that you need to be united and to stick together, affirming and acting upon the principle that you should not allow any schisms, divisions, or factions to develop between yourselves. Instead, I urge you to be committed to standing shoulder to shoulder and acting together with a shared and single-minded determination and purpose.[19]

Different roles don't mean we need to have different agendas. It is true that God has designed us with distinct roles and responsibilities by making some of us people who start new things with vision and passion because of the resurrected Jesus; giving some of us the ability to share His heart in a powerful way, both for what is happening now and what will happen in the future; gifting some of us with a passion to reach people who are not yet followers of Jesus with the incredibly positive, powerful, and life-transforming message of who Jesus is and why He came; and enabling some of us to shepherd those God entrusts to us by protecting them, guiding them, instructing them – tenderly, clearly, and strongly – and setting them an example in our own priorities and conduct. All these roles combine with one clear, united aim and purpose, though, which is to prepare, train, and release Christ's holy followers to get on with the task of serving God by serving His powerful purposes in the world. Whatever our role might be, we are all called to demonstrate Christ's values and priorities by living as His servants ourselves, and to give our energy and passion to strengthening, increasing, and honouring Christ's very body on earth, the family of God that we call the church. We are to persevere at this magnificent task until the unity that He has given us in principle is clearly demonstrated in the way we think, the way we behave, and the way we treat one another.

This unity is deeply embedded in the truth of who Jesus is and what He has done, and in the purposes of God for us. The more clearly we understand Jesus and the closer we come to who He is, why He came, and what He has done, the more powerfully we will demonstrate this principle of standing together and serving together. That is because we will fundamentally understand that because of who the Son of God is and what He has done for us, we are immeasurably stronger together than we are on our own. As we step into this powerful unity we will learn to straighten our backs and walk with greater confidence and courage, looking resolutely into the world around us with the same boldness of heart and gravitas as our Saviour Himself did.[20]

It is as clear as the nose on one another's faces that we need each other. The different parts of a body have different functions to fulfil but they are all needed. The same is true of us. If we forget that we will never stay united.[21]

It is not always easy to get along, so we have to learn to put up with one another, and we can only do that with God's help. Putting up with one another means we have to learn to first allow God to work through us, then we have to learn the art of standing together and getting along better. That means that even when someone has a legitimate reason for being unhappy with someone else in the family we have to deal with it properly and learn what it means to cancel the debt caused by the situation and be gracious, kind, and forgiving toward one another.

The foundation for that course of action is to simply remember that you need to learn to treat other people the way Jesus has treated you. He has been gracious, kind, and compassionate to you and cancelled your debt to Him by forgiving you. The incredible flow of His forgiveness to you is not supposed to stop with you; it is supposed to flow through you to one another. This is not an optional extra. It is a fundamental part of being in God's family. To make this way of life a priority, you need to dress yourself in unconditional, accepting, and welcoming love. That is the same kind of love that Jesus has shown to you. Only that kind of love can hold you together as God's people. Without it you will sound like an orchestra that is out of tune, but with it you will make the most remarkable and attractive sound together. With this kind of love the symphony of your lives will be utterly faultless and you will sound pitch-perfect to a world that is yearning for good music.[22]

This sense of being a deeply united family is the heartbeat of what Jesus Himself asked His Father for. His prayer for this is breathtaking in its scope. He didn't only want this kind of togetherness for those who were His contemporary followers; He also wanted it for those of us who have come into the family and acknowledged Jesus as our Lord and our Head because of the words that His contemporaries have spoken. Our spiritual life and priorities flow directly from Jesus' contemporary followers and we therefore share their spiritual DNA. That is why we feel the impact of His prayer. Jesus wants us all to be united, to be one family. He doesn't want a single one of His family to be left out. There is no one anywhere in the family of God who should feel isolated, cut off, or as if they are not part of His body.

The unity and singleness of heart, mind, and purpose Jesus wants for us has its deep roots in who God Himself is. The relationship between Jesus and His Father is the source and the symbol of the kind of relationships that Jesus wants us to have with God and with one another. The roots of our lives need to be deeply embedded in who God is, what God has done for us, and what He wants to do among us and through us. And the purpose of this togetherness and unity is absolutely clear.

It isn't just so we can be happy. Our unity and togetherness is not an end itself. Our unity, togetherness, and singleness of heart demonstrate to the world around us that Jesus was who He claimed to be. Our unity is a magnet that draws people to Jesus and is one of the core ways in which the world around us comes to understand that Jesus truly is the Messiah, the Saviour of the world, and that the Father sent Him to the world to rescue, redeem, and renew us.

The astounding thing is that Jesus has already given us the very same splendour and brilliance that He enjoys with His Father. It is not something that He plans to give us at some point in the future. He has already given it to us. That glorious, shimmering brilliance is like a magnet that draws us to one another, and the closer we come to one another, the more brightly we shine. The gift of His glory in us has a knock-on effect. This gift to us is supposed to make us increasingly realize that we are already connected to one another. Our practice of unity has to follow the reality of the gift of unity we have already been given.

The more brightly we shine, the more attractive we appear to others. Actually, what is attractive to others is the brilliance and the shimmering beauty of Jesus in us individually and, more powerfully, in us collectively. Jesus reiterates this reality forcefully for us as He prays. He wants us to understand and be shaped by the abiding and constant reality that He has already given us His presence. It is His presence rather than simply our effort that is the basis of our shared life, shared identity, and shared purpose. Our unity is nothing more and nothing less than a mirror of the unity between the Father and the Son. His gift of unity to us is utterly comprehensive, impacting every single part of our understanding of ourselves, of others in the family, and of our place and purpose in the world around us.

God has done it this way for a reason. He wants the world around us to see beautiful, purposeful, life-giving relationships and to realize that He Himself is beautiful, purposeful, and life-giving. As the world around us sees this kind of common life and common purpose it is drawn toward the reality that God has a common life and common purpose and has shown it to us in sending the Lord Jesus to the earth. As they see this they realize that it is love that sits at the heart of God's character and actions. Love unites the Father and the Son. The same love unites God and His people. The same love unites His people with one another. The same love flows from His people to those who are not yet His people.[23]

The beauty of such unity automatically captures the attention of others. It is dazzlingly attractive and inherently good. It has a positive and affirming impact on those who see it. It has an even greater impact on those who experience it. It can be enjoyed in the same way as the beautiful scent of a garden that is full of different flowers. Such a garden can produce a magnificent and attractive aroma. To put it another way, it can be experienced like the wonderful atmosphere at a party where there are lots of different people yet everyone is having fun. Alternatively, it can be tasted in the same way that all the ingredients that go into a beautiful meal can be when they combine to make one unforgettable tasting experience. The challenging thing is that flowers take time to grow together, friendships and relationships develop over different shared experiences, and the best-tasting meals take time to cook so that the flavours can mingle together slowly.

The same is true of the unity that God has given us. Although it is His gift to us, it becomes more visible to others and more enjoyable to all the longer we ourselves enjoy it, commit to it, and live in it. As we give it our time and attention, this sense of common purpose, common identity, and common heart becomes like an incredibly attractive cologne or perfume that has drenched us. I'm not talking about a little hint of the scent here and there. I mean it feels like the whole bottle has been poured over us and the scent is infusing the air both far and wide. Such a committed and consistent approach to unity soaks those who experience it with life, refreshment, and vitality. It's like a daily deluge of God's provision and blessing, like a mist of mercy or a staggering, breath-taking sunrise of grace for all who experience it. When we live in the reality of this gift of unity we experience a continual sense of blessing, life, peace, and purpose. Not only that, the world around us also experiences the same powerful benefits.[24]

These immense benefits of unity are the bedrock of why we need to make it a central principle of our own lives both individually and together. We need to make it a priority to have relationships that go beyond superficiality and instead develop habits and attitudes that are conduits for the unity God has already given us. We share life together, not just meetings, because we share a common purpose, a common identity, and a common destiny. We are in this thing called "life" together. We are in God's family together. We endure hardships together and we celebrate joys together: at least we are supposed to. The unity God has given us means we can see the difficulties that others in the family face and we can be determined to walk with them rather than just watch them from a distance. Our love is the love of siblings who are utterly committed to one another. Our hearts can be soft, compassionate, and gentle toward one another and we can believe the best of one another, not the worst. So this unity impacts our intentions, our decisions, our responses, our affections, our emotions, and our attitudes.[25]

This way of life takes a determined and clear decision. It demands consistent, intentional attitudes of grace and humility to protect our core convictions around a shared identity, purpose, and destiny. Not only that, but we also need to remind ourselves constantly that protecting the strong ties of unity produces a deep awareness of the whole well-being that God provides to His people, and therefore it is worth the effort.[26]

The world around us has not seen God. They do not know what He looks like or what He sounds like. They have never met Him on the street. That is not their fault. No one has ever seen God directly like this. When we learn to live in the unity that He has given us, however, those around us see God very clearly in us. They see and experience His love as they see that we love one another. As we make the love and the purpose of God our aim and objective in life, other people see Him in our actions, our attitudes, and our character. The clearest way they see that in our lives is in how we treat one another in the family. When we love one another we are showing that His love is not just a theory but it is also a practical, life-transforming reality in our lives. If God can enable us to love one another with such depth, then He can also help others who have never experienced such love to experience it too. Our togetherness of heart and purpose then becomes a window through which others can see God Himself.[27]

This togetherness can be seen in the way we treat those who are different from us, and it demands a response of humility and grace in us. We should not only spend time with those we like; those who are like us, or those who share our social, political, or cultural outlook. We should not only spend time with those who agree with us! Instead, we need to find ways of putting aside such presumptuous and prideful barriers and self-imposed fences and give our energy to making every possible effort to spend time with those who appear to be somehow less than we are. We need to be careful not to think we are cleverer than others, better than others, wiser than others, or more important than others. An honest and humble understanding of ourselves will help us to relate to others in a much more Christlike way. We need to be careful not to become too big for our boots.[28]

Perhaps we would do well to remember that we are all still learning? Not one of us is a professional or an expert when it comes to believing; instead we are all lifelong students. Unity is strengthened by humility, and humility is easier when we remember that there is only one perfect teacher for us as Christians: His name is Jesus. We are all His followers, first and foremost.[29]

There is good reason for giving Him this central place in our lives and in our commitment to a shared identity, purpose, and destiny. He is the Only One who is able to provide us with a deep sense of connectedness to God and therefore to each other. He is the only one who reconnected us with God and the whole-life peace that God gives us. It was His physical, flesh-and-bone life, His suffering, and His violent death that not only reconnected us with God but also connected us with one another. He Himself removed the enmity, suspicion, and hatred that once locked us into our own narrow points of view and away from other people and their perspectives. He is the Source of our unity together because He is the Source of connection with God and with God's peace.[30]

We have the perfect example to follow, therefore, in our commitment to a shared identity, purpose, and destiny. All the encouragement we need for a deeper commitment to these things is seen in Christ Himself. He provides us with the perfect example of love. By doing so, He inspires us to be like Him in the way we love others. His openness to and dependence upon the Holy Spirit shows us that our commitment to unity is only possible by that same openness and dependence. By looking at the way Jesus thought, lived, and taught we ourselves can become more committed to the kind of togetherness that creates a deep sense of connectedness, understanding, and heartfelt empathy and compassion for others in the Christian family.[31] We stand as siblings in the family of God with our common link being what Jesus Christ has done *for* us and what He has done *in* us. As we recognize His centrality and allow our thinking and actions to be shaped by what

He has done for us, we are not only clearer about ourselves but we are also able to treat one another as equals in a better way.

When we were baptized we were plunged into Jesus' death and resurrection. In that moment we were stripped of all the previous trappings of how we understood ourselves. Once we have gone through that public rite, stating we belong to Jesus and to His family, we are dressed in Him. That means, in effect, what previously defined us is now irrelevant because He is now the One who defines us. The impact of that is that He not only defines us personally, He also defines how we see one another. Old racial, ethnic, religious, and spiritual dividing lines are destroyed when we become part of Jesus' family. Just as these things are irrelevant, so is our social and economic standing. It doesn't matter whether we are rich or we are poor. It doesn't matter whether someone has more freedom or less freedom than we do. It doesn't even matter any more whether we are male or female. These things have not changed, but the way they define us has! The only thing that matters now is how God defines us. How He defines us shapes how we define ourselves and how we define other people. The basis for those definitions is not what we once were but instead it is what we have become in Jesus Christ. He is both the yardstick of our own lives and the bond that exists between us and the rest of the family.[32]

Our unity flows from Him because He is the Source of our shared identity, purpose, and destiny. Our life flows from Him. Our purpose flows from Him. Our future flows from Him. We are organically and permanently connected to Him because He is the head of our family. That also means that we are organically and permanently connected to all other Christians because we are all part of one body and He is the head of that body. Our connection with Him automatically creates our connection with all other Christians. He is the beating heart at the centre of this body called the church. We are completely and utterly dependent upon His Spirit flowing into us and through us into the family and the wider world. Nothing can change that. The question is whether we are blocking the flow of His Spirit or participating with that flow. Our unity is experienced more deeply when we remember that we are already connected because of what the Father, the Son, and the Holy Spirit have done for us, are doing in us, and will do for us in the future.[33]

So please remember that unity is not something we strive for; it is something we have already been given. It flows from Jesus and what He has done for us. We are His body, organically and permanently connected to Him and therefore intimately, organically, and permanently connected to one another. Every time something happens in God's family in one place, it affects the whole family. We are a single unit, and out of the realization that we are a single unit flows the fuller and deeper experience of our unity. Each of us has a responsibility to find out where we fit in this single unit and then play our part by being connected and committed to Christ and by being connected and committed to one another. If every person who is part of God's family were to behave in this way, there would be no stopping us. We would grow more. We would reach further. We would be more effective. We would love more deeply.[34]

It's worth emphasizing once again that our common identity, common purpose, and common destiny are deeply rooted in what Jesus has already done for us. We are directly connected to Him and to one another in His death and therefore we are directly connected to Him and to one another in our destiny. It is because Jesus has already been resurrected that we have such a common destiny. One day, all of God's people will reign with Him. This is a certainty that is secured by Christ's death and life. Our unity is not something we hope for in the future. It is something already given to us by Jesus that will be displayed more and more fully as time passes. We have a shared future because we share a Saviour.[35]

So let me repeat what I said in the first place. I am pleading with you with all the passion, intensity, and authority that Jesus has given me and because we are each under His Lordship and therefore irrevocably connected to one another. I beg you to recognize that you need to be united and stick together, affirming and acting upon the principle that you should not allow any schisms, divisions, or factions to develop between yourselves. Instead, I urge you to be committed to standing shoulder to shoulder and acting together with a shared and single-minded determination and purpose.[36]

Amen.

"In Him"

Our identity sets the tone for the type of person we are and how we will treat other people. If we live out of a primary identity as followers of Christ as Baptist or Pentecostals or Anglicans or Roman Catholics or any other denominational tag, then we will find church unity much harder than it needs to be. One of the biggest challenges that local churches face when it comes to making unity work in their community is the underlying assumptions that followers of Jesus hold about other Christians. We can reveal a great deal about these assumptions in the way we talk about Christians from other churches. I remember a conversation with a couple who had decided to plant a new church in a particular part of their local community. They outlined all the reasons why none of the churches in that area were any good and why they, and they alone, were going to be used by God to bring new life and new hope to the community. It may well have been that God was calling them to plant a new church, and that He wanted to bless them and to multiply them, but they had fallen into the trap of defining themselves and their ministry through how popular they were and how effective they were being rather than through their identity in Christ.

Our ministries and our churches are never about us. We are not the centre of the Christian community – Christ is. Our churches will not be able to work well with other local expressions of the body of Christ until we have helped them to understand that they do not need to be defined by comparison with other churches. A local church's identity does not come from how big it is in comparison to the other churches in the community; instead it flows from its people understanding who they are *in Christ*. Our effectiveness is not about our size; it is about our faithfulness to what God has called us to be.

I have learned an incredibly important lesson in my pastoral ministry over the thirty years that I have been involved in leading churches. I do not need to pull others apart in order to step in to the future and the purposes that God has for me. If I begin to define myself by the success or failure of other people and other ministries, then I will quickly descend into emotional uncertainty, spiritual pride or jealousy (because one is the flip side of the other), and leadership insecurity. I will begin to treat the local church that I lead as if it is my possession, and the people in it as if they owe me a greater degree of loyalty than they do Christ. I will become suspicious of them when they don't do what I want, and if they ever leave the local church that I lead, I will take it as a personal insult. Without a clear sense of both my identity being in Christ and the identity of the people whom I pastor being in Christ, I will always be suspicious of other local churches. Unhealthy comparison kills healthy collaboration.

Not only that, but if I place too much emphasis on what I believe and what I want, I elevate myself to a platform that God does not want me to have. Pastors with insecure identity issues create church cultures where believers become afraid of reaching out to other Christians in their area. If we want our churches to be communities that are genuinely able to celebrate what God is doing in each of our expressions of faith, we have to find a way to rediscover the reality that our primary identity is found in who we are in Christ.[37] If we lack a core understanding of our identity in Christ we will end up looking over our shoulders suspiciously at other churches in our community, and we will also end up looking over our shoulders suspiciously at people in our own church. Not only will this insecurity create division between churches, it will also create division within our own church, because we will feel that our popularity is the platform for our identity, and the support of our church members will be the source of our spiritual strength. When that happens, division, suspicion, and factions are just round the corner. A prime example of that is the church in Corinth.

Personality cults and private agendas

The ancient city of Corinth lies about forty-eight miles west of Athens on the narrow stretch of land that joins the Peloponnesian peninsula to mainland Greece. Today it is the second largest city in the region, but when Paul wrote to its inhabitants, probably around AD 53–55, it was a bustling metropolis that oversaw trade from the Adriatic and the Aegean Seas. It was a hotbed of ideas. Temples were everywhere, but none was as grand as the huge temple to Diana, and they came with a rainbow of practices and priorities. Pausanias, a second-century author, wrote about the city, and his words read like a lonely-planet guide to pagan monumental sacred sites.[38]

Among its many shrines, the city boasted an important shrine to Asclepius, the god of healing. Sexual ethics were liberal – the city was known for its wanton sexual practices

– and this metropolis was pulsating with diverse social backgrounds, cultures, ethnicities, and ideas. The city was alive with the arguments and counter-arguments of a wide range of philosophies from Stoicism[39] to Cynicism.[40] It was the home of the Isthmian Games[41] every two years. It was also the home of a Christian community that was marked by division and disagreement over a whole range of issues. Those issues, perhaps not surprisingly, reflected the culture of the wider community into which the church had been born, and included sexual ethics, the role and place of women, how the Holy Spirit moved, and ideas about who was most important in the church community there.[42] The church was riven with personality cults and personal agendas. It was breaking under the pressure of internal schisms and arguments.

In his first letter to the Corinthian church, Paul reminds them that they are not defined by the leaders of the present moment but are rather defined by their position in Christ:

> For as long as there is jealousy and quarrelling among you, are you not of the flesh, and behaving according to human inclinations? For when one says, "I belong to Paul", and another, "I belong to Apollos", are you not merely human?
>
> What then is Apollos? What is Paul? Servants through whom you came to believe, as the Lord assigned to each. I planted, Apollos watered, but God gave the growth. So neither the one who plants nor the one who waters is anything, but only God who gives the growth. The one who plants and the one who waters have a common purpose, and each will receive wages according to the labour of each. For we are God's servants, working together; you are God's field, God's building…

So let no one boast about human leaders. For all things are yours, whether Paul or Apollos or Cephas or the world or life or death or the present or the future – all belong to you, and you belong to Christ, and Christ belongs to God.

1 Corinthians 3:3b–9, 21–23

On the surface, their divisions and their disagreements appear to be because of their strong personalities and their strong views. This is no doubt true for them, as it is for us, at least in part, when our disagreements define us more than our common life. Paul's solution, however, is simple. Before he challenges their behaviours he reminds them of the common source of their identity: they are Christ's. It is their identity in the Lord Jesus that gives them definition, personally and together. They are wrong in allowing their secondary allegiances, to Paul or Cephas or Apollos, to become primary allegiances. Not only that, but Paul goes on to demonstrate to them that he is able to withstand their criticisms and the attacks and criticisms of others because he has a deep awareness of his identity and his purpose in Christ:

We are fools for the sake of Christ, but you are wise in Christ. We are weak, but you are strong. You are held in honour, but we in disrepute. To the present hour we are hungry and thirsty, we are poorly clothed and beaten and homeless, and we grow weary from the work of our own hands. When reviled, we bless; when persecuted, we endure; when slandered, we speak kindly. We have become like the rubbish of the world, the dregs of all things, to this very day.

1 Corinthians 4:10–13

Paul is not asking the Corinthian Christians to take their identity from Christ while he takes his identity from his role or his position within the Christian community. Instead, he applies exactly the same principles to them as he applies to himself. Just as he is defined by who he is in Christ, so they are defined by who they are in Christ. Paul can only address issues of conflict, schism, and disagreement with them after he has asserted their central identity in Christ. In fact, at the beginning of 1 Corinthians 4, Paul makes it very clear that he has a deep sense of his identity springing from Christ:

> *But with me it is a very small thing that I should be judged by you or by any human court. I do not even judge myself. I am not aware of anything against myself, but I am not thereby acquitted. It is the Lord who judges me.*
>
> 1 Corinthians 4:3–4

Paul has little to no concern about what they think of him, precisely because he is aware that his primary definition is found through who Christ is and what Christ has done in him.

In another of his letters, that to the Philippians, Paul makes this point even more clearly. He sets out his rich heritage and the deep traditions from which he has emerged, then proceeds to say that they amount to nothing compared to who he is in Christ and what Christ has done in him:

> *Beware of the dogs, beware of the evil workers, beware of those who mutilate the flesh! For it is we who are the circumcision, who worship in the Spirit of God and boast in Christ Jesus and have no confidence in the flesh – even though I, too, have reason for confidence in the flesh.*

If anyone else has reason to be confident in the flesh, I have more: circumcised on the eighth day, a member of the people of Israel, of the tribe of Benjamin, a Hebrew born of Hebrews; as to the law, a Pharisee; as to zeal, a persecutor of the church; as to righteousness under the law, blameless.

Yet whatever gains I had, these I have come to regard as loss because of Christ. More than that, I regard everything as loss because of the surpassing value of knowing Christ Jesus my Lord. For his sake I have suffered the loss of all things, and I regard them as rubbish, in order that I may gain Christ and be found in him, not having a righteousness of my own that comes from the law, but one that comes through faith in Christ, the righteousness from God based on faith. I want to know Christ and the power of his resurrection and the sharing of his sufferings by becoming like him in his death, if somehow I may attain the resurrection from the dead.

Philippians 3:2–11

Paul is able to rise above the accusations and small-mindedness of those around him precisely because he has a strong sense of his identity and purpose in Christ. In verse 3 he notes that he will boast "in Christ". In verse 7 he makes it clear that everything else sits behind who he is in Christ. In verse 8 he describes knowing Christ as of "surpassing value", and he displays a deep yearning and passion for Christ because his deepest desire, according to verse 9, is to be found "in him, not having a righteousness of my own that comes from the law, but one that comes through faith in Christ, the righteousness from God based on faith."

The first building block of Christian unity in us and in our churches is to understand that the reality of being in Christ comes before anything and everything else. This is not some kind of theological principle that sits detached from our daily lives. It is only as we allow this truth to sink deep into our souls that we can begin to see ourselves, and consequently other people, differently. We will never achieve Christian unity at the level that God desires for us if we cannot first see who we are in Christ and who Christ is in us. In Christ we have been given grace, before the world began.[43] In Christ we were chosen before the foundation of the world.[44] In Christ we are deeply and continually loved with a love that cannot be broken.[45] In Christ we have been totally accepted, redeemed, and forgiven.[46] In Christ we are not only forgiven, we are also justified and given the righteousness of God in exchange for the brokenness and sin of our own lives.[47] We are part of a new creation in Christ, given a new identity and therefore a new perspective and new purpose.[48] We become part of a new family in Christ, which is not defined by our ancestry but by His blood. We are now clothed with Christ and our primary identity is not in our cultural status (Jew or Gentile), our economic status (slave or free), or our gender (male or female). Instead we are united together in Christ:

> Now before faith came, we were imprisoned and guarded under the law until faith would be revealed. Therefore the law was our disciplinarian until Christ came, so that we might be justified by faith. But now that faith has come, we are no longer subject to a disciplinarian, for in Christ Jesus you are all children of God through faith. As many of you as were baptized into Christ have clothed yourselves with Christ. There is no longer Jew or Greek, there is no longer slave or free, there is no longer male and female; for all of you are

one in Christ Jesus. And if you belong to Christ, then you are
Abraham's offspring, heirs according to the promise.

Galatians 3:23–29

We are seated with God in Christ and now share both a privileged position and a special perspective.[49] We can stand in the power and the provision of all that God has done for us in Christ because He is the security and the seal of every promise of God.[50] It is our position in Christ and Christ's work in us that makes us holy and sanctifies us.[51] It is in Christ that our real needs can be met.[52] It is in Christ that we find peace of heart and peace of mind.[53] It is in and through Christ that we discover a quality of life that is so far beyond our understanding that the Bible describes it as eternal life.[54] Our hope of life after death and permanent union with God is in Christ and in what He has done for us in the resurrection.[55] It is little wonder, then, that the American pastor John Piper has described our position in Christ as a "stupendous reality".[56] This foundational reality of who we are in Christ is so important to the issue of unity. If we cannot define ourselves by who God has made us, then we will also fail to define other Christians properly. The failure to understand our Christian identity is, I am convinced, at the root of almost every pastoral crisis that I have encountered that involves conflict with another Christian. The failure to be shaped by who we are in Christ will lead us into separation and isolation because we will not be sufficiently confident of who we are in God to enable us to engage with other people. A lack of this confident identity in Christ will either make us hyper-sensitive to the opinions of others because of a chronic lack of identity, or it will lead us to constantly strive for the approval of others because we have not yet discovered our approval in God.

A personal story of how this reality transformed my life

I was converted to Christ when I was sixteen years old when I lived in Belfast. For a complex series of reasons, I had a deep sense of worthlessness about myself. I constantly needed the approval of others. For the first five years of my Christian life, I sought the approval of men and women everywhere I went and in everything I did. When I was seventeen I went to live in Mexico for a period of time and worked in an orphanage. I thought I had found a place where I could be loved and accepted, but the reality was that I had simply masked my lack of identity in Christ by ministering to a group of boys and girls who needed me. Their need of me was what defined me. I returned to the United Kingdom and moved to Scotland, where I became involved in planting a church. I loved it. I found a deep sense of community in the church and felt like I was part of something. However, there was still a deep lack in me that I was not letting God minister into. I still desperately needed the approval of other people. This had two effects on my life.

Firstly, I became more and more critical of other people. In reality, I was jealous of them and I could not cope with anyone else receiving praise or commendation while I was still struggling with my own lack of confidence. No one around me would ever have guessed this was how I felt because on the outside I presented as very together and very self-assured. On the inside, however, I was desperate for approval. In order to try to obtain that approval I became more and more dependent upon the affirmation and encouragement of those who were in authority over me. Pastors, youth pastors, leaders, bosses, and even friends were people whom I longed to please not because I loved them (although it was true that I did love them), but because I needed them to love me *and to tell me that they did*. I would try to prove my spiritual stamina, astuteness, and strength by becoming more and more vociferous about people in other churches and from other traditions whose lifestyles or attitudes or beliefs did not chime with ours. In other words, my lack of confidence in who I was in Christ made me more and more critical of who other people were in Christ. In my desperation to be affirmed, I was ready to criticize other people. In order to feel loved, I was ready to reject other people. The irony and tragedy of that, as I read the words on the page in front of me, are heartbreaking. I was constantly shunning the very community that could give me love because I wanted so deeply to be loved that I would hurt others to experience that love.

The second impact was that I was deeply driven. I play the clarinet and the saxophone. I needed to be affirmed in my playing – all the time. When I preached, I needed others to tell me how good it was. If I prayed in public – and I did that a lot – I wanted others to tell me how anointed my prayer was, how powerful it was. I never missed a meeting at church because I wanted the affirmation of my fellow leaders. I volunteered for everything in the hope that I would be affirmed. All this was happening right under the noses of my friends and my fellow leaders and no one ever attempted to help me understand the reasons for my behaviour. No one sat down with me to talk to me about my driven lifestyle. When an international evangelist came to Scotland, I volunteered to help with the mission. I was working full-time in a paid job too. For three weeks I survived on fifteen minutes of sleep here and there. I worked all day in the office, then sang in the choir of the crusade, then helped with counselling new believers, then volunteered in the office through the night sorting and sifting the decision cards and praying for each person whose card I held in my hands. The pressure was intense, but I did it all because I wanted approval. It left me ill, hospitalized, and uncertain about my future, but I still sought the approval of others.

Then, months later, everything changed, because God met me at the deepest point of my need. I attended a concert in Motherwell where the Christian singer Larry Norman was performing. In the middle of one of his songs he stopped and spoke to the audience. He said something that God used to change my life. He told us that there was nothing we could do to make God love us any more deeply and that there was nothing that we could do to make God love us any less deeply than God did at that moment. He then said that God would never be disillusioned with us because He never had any illusions about us in the first place. The words exploded in my head like a volcano of love and grace and I started to sob. I felt like I couldn't stop crying. In fact, I cried for three weeks. I'd wake up crying and then I'd go to bed crying and I would cry all day in between. I had never experienced anything like this before, and I have never experienced anything like it since. In the midst of it, however, I knew what God was doing.

God was reaching into the very heart of a confused, desperate young man with a self-esteem that was on the floor, and He was transforming me. He was pulling out all the hurt, rejection, pain, and fear I had felt all my life and was replacing them with His healing, His acceptance, His comfort, and the gift of faith. He was bringing the reality of who I am in Christ into the very heart of my understanding of God, of myself, and of my place in the world. He was destroying my need for the approval of others, and with it the criticisms of others, the driven nature of my life, and the constant unhappiness I felt about myself.

After three weeks the crying stopped. Up until this episode, every morning of my life I would look in the mirror and whisper to my reflection that I was ugly, that I was stupid, and that if something went wrong that day it would be my fault. On the morning that the crying stopped, I went to the mirror in the bathroom and looked at myself and I thought, for the first time in my life, that I was loved and I was accepted – and I was not stupid.

From that moment twenty-six years ago until today, I have been far less concerned about what other people think of me. Of course, there have been moments when that desire to be affirmed has raised its head in unhealthy ways, but it has happened very rarely. Instead, for the last twenty-six years I have enjoyed a security in God's love for me that has transformed me. It has made me less critical of others. It has taken away my need to be right. It has enabled me to see the beauty of what God is doing in other people's lives and ministries without becoming jealous or critical. It has given me the freedom to appreciate the wider body of Christ, and it has enabled me to live, largely, free of fear, free of the need to manipulate other people's emotions, and free of the need to win the favour or the affirmation of others.

In Him we live and move and have our being

As we discover who we are in Christ, we are able to celebrate who others are in Christ. If you are a pastor or a leader of a local church and you are struggling to unite the church you lead, then start here. Teach it, model it, pray it, sing it; do whatever you need to do to get this truth into the hearts and the minds of your church family. Get on your knees and ask God to give your church a new understanding of their identity in Christ. I would encourage you to model it too. If you haven't discovered this life-changing assurance, then you will always be on your guard about how to deal with other churches and you will always take it personally when people leave your church. The root of your identity lies in what you do rather than in Whose you are. We can find freedom in Christ and in Christ alone. It is only, in the words of the Apostle Paul, who was himself quoting a poet of his day, when we discover that in Christ "we live and move and have our being"[57] that we can find the freedom to love other people too.

Over the years I have had the privilege of leading in two wonderful organizations. One was the Evangelical Alliance, where I was Head of Church and Mission. I was responsible for leading the Alliance's work with thousands of churches. The second was Faithworks, a Christian social action advocacy group that worked with churches across the United Kingdom. In both roles, I was given the opportunity to meet Christians from streams and traditions that were not my normal environment. In the years that I led in those organizations, I was given the joy of discovering the beauty of the breadth and the depth of God's family. God has His people, who are "in Him", everywhere! Once we discover that we are in Christ, we have the privilege of seeing Christ in so many other believers. It's like walking into a room full of family that you have never met.

I led Spring Harvest from 2012 to 2017 and continue to be part of the leadership team of that event and the theologian-in-residence for the overarching charity, Essential Christian. I have been involved with Spring Harvest since 2002. In the fifteen years of my involvement with that festival, I have discovered so many beautiful Christians from streams and backgrounds and traditions that I was once wary of. I delight in the connection that comes from discovering what it means to be in Christ.

In most of our communities, although by no means all, there are men and women and young people who know and love Jesus and who belong to a different part of the church family than we do. We are not united by the many different expressions of tradition, style, or doctrinal deviations and differences that we hold. There is only one thing that truly and powerfully unites us. We were bought with the same blood. We were baptized into the same family. We hold to the same Lord. We are each given the same Spirit. We share a common identity in the one Father. We are committed to the one Faith. We have a common hope.

When Paul wrote to the Ephesians, he urged them to keep this in mind and to keep at the work of loving one another and serving one another. He wanted them to keep the main thing as the main thing. Perhaps we would do well to do the same. It will mean we need to learn to disagree well, to listen more than we talk, and to be willing to see Christ in someone else – but this is the only way to genuine, heartfelt, God-honouring unity. Christian unity starts and ends with what God has done for us, not what we can do for Him. May God help us to centre all of our thoughts, actions, and intentions around being united in the reality that this unity already exists – and it includes every single person through time and history who has been brought into the family of God through Christ and what He has done for each one of us individually. If

God calls them son or daughter, we have only one option – they are our brothers and sisters.

> *I therefore, the prisoner in the Lord, beg you to lead a life worthy of the calling to which you have been called, with all humility and gentleness, with patience, bearing with one another in love, making every effort to maintain the unity of the Spirit in the bond of peace. There is one body and one Spirit, just as you were called to the one hope of your calling, one Lord, one faith, one baptism, one God and Father of all, who is above all and through all and in all.*
>
> Ephesians 4:1–6

Protecting Unity

Recognizing the fact of profound impact within the church, can we find a way together to make the manner of our encounter with each other a gift to a broken world, and not a scandal?[58]

That Christians disagree with each other is an inevitability, that we reject one another is a choice. Perhaps it is an inevitability that people who feel passionately about something will end up disagreeing passionately too. Our history of disagreement, as the church, is not exactly a shining example to the world of how to love one another through our arguments, our spats, and our divisions. Throughout the story of the bride of Christ, we have been rather too quick to turn our backs on one another and rather too slow to find a way of loving one another more deeply despite the differences that we face.

One example of strong disagreement and sharp use of language is the reformer Martin Luther. His works are scattered with dismissive comments and famous insults to his opponents such as this, written in his "Against the Roman Papacy, an Institution of the Devil":

Even if we were stones and wooden blocks, we could see by your works throughout all the world that you are lost, desperate children of the devil and also mad, crude asses in

Scripture. Someone probably would like to curse you so that you might be struck down by lightning and thunder, burned by hellish fire, have the plague, syphilis, epilepsy, the plague of St. Anthony, leprosy, carbuncles, and all the plagues – but these are all caresses, and God has long ago punished you with greater plagues, just like God's despisers and blasphemers should be punished.[59]

Of course, we must remember that Luther was a child of his time. The invective that flowed between him and Pope Leo X was laced with accusations in the form of simile, metaphor, and insult. It has to be said, though, that Luther's language seems to have been strong no matter who he was challenging.[60]

Many followers of Christ have been guilty of bad disagreement. If it were simply that we were guilty of the use of heated language the issue would be less serious, but that is not the case. Theological and ecclesiological disagreements have gone much further and caused much more pain.

At their worst... theological disagreements between professing Christians have led beyond violent speech and personal insults to physical intimidation, exile, and imprisonment, even to brutal torture and execution. Five Archbishops of Canterbury have died violently, lynched by the mob, burned at the stake or beheaded by the axe-man, which has prompted the current archbishop, Justin Welby, to reflect that, mercifully, the worst he has to face is "execution by the daily newspapers".[61]

Some of the divisions in the church are rooted deeply in our history. I remember my first visit to Jerusalem and the Church of the Holy Sepulchre. I was deeply troubled by the conflict between the denominations that share ownership of that site and the way they treated one another. During my visit I was astounded to witness a moment when a procession from one denomination came face to face with a procession from another and they began to hurl insults at one another and jostle with one another. In fact, the keys to the church have been held by a Muslim family for around 1,000 years because the Christians do not trust one another with them.

Other conflicts are more modern, and take a more modern form. You only need to browse the internet for a few moments to find the hurtful, unkind, and aggressive ways in which Christians speak to one another in the blogosphere.

> *Professing Christians seem to have an endless capacity for caustic commentary, character assassination, mutual suspicion, and the gushing forth of vitriol, which are signs of a distressing spiritual malaise.*[62]

The truth still matters, but so does grace

We don't need to rehearse any further the details of the disagreements we have had through the centuries as Christians. Any attempt to do so would fill several thousand pages and still only scratch the surface. In our generation, the church of Jesus Christ faces deep challenges over the way we relate to one another. Surely there can be no doubt that the way we speak to one another and the way we treat one another is a scandal? We cannot preach a message of love, hope, forgiveness, and tenderness to the world then treat each other with such contempt. The world watches how we behave toward one another, and I have no doubt that our example often puts them off. There has to be a better way.[63]

In seeking to find that better way, however, we need to be careful to avoid the trap of making disagreement something to be avoided at all costs. Truth matters. We do not protect unity by avoiding the hard questions. Far too much talk of unity across churches today is maintained by simply avoiding the hard conversations. That cannot be the right way forward. A unity that is paper thin cannot stand the winds of adversity. To borrow an image from the Sermon on the Mount, if we build our unity on sand, when the tide comes in, what we have built will be washed away:

> "Everyone then who hears these words of mine and acts on them will be like a wise man who built his house on rock. The rain fell, the floods came, and the winds blew and beat on that house, but it did not fall, because it had been founded on rock. And everyone who hears these words of mine and does not act on them will be like a foolish man who built his house on sand. The rain fell, and the floods came, and the winds blew and beat against that house, and it fell – and great was its fall!"
>
> Matthew 7:24–27

Weak unity or avoided conflict does not help the witness of the church in the world, and it does not last. Instead, we need to find a way of conversing with one another which puts the anchors of truth and grace at the centre of our relationships. What Christ has said and what He has taught us matters very deeply. Our unity must surely be built around His words. There are several layers of this for me.

How do I handle unity as a pastor?

As a pastor, I often find myself in situations where I have to say something that is hard. It feels like those situations come at me from every direction. As the leader of a congregation, it is my responsibility to guide people into a deeper relationship with God and a better understanding of His love for them and of His purposes for them in the world. As an evangelical, my understanding of how I do that is to see them ever more deeply rooted in the truth of Scripture, and my prayer is that they will allow the Jesus of Scripture to shape their personal and their public choices.

It isn't long before that commitment is tested. What do I say to the young couple who come to me to tell me that they want to live together before they are married? How do I handle the questions from a member of my congregation when they tell me that they have been to a conference where they were told that everyone should be healed? How do I handle the passionate Christian who comes into my study and asks me if the God of the Old Testament is a different God to the God of the New Testament? And what about the man who sits with me in a coffee shop and tells me that he has fallen out of love with his wife and wants to move on to a new relationship, and then tells me that he can't help who he falls in love with? And of course, there is the question that many pastors struggle with: what do you do when two men or two women tell you that they love one another and want to get married and they want you to conduct the ceremony?[64]

How do I handle unity as a leader in our church family?

The ecclesiology of the local church that I lead is one of eldership. I am called to lead the church and to lead the eldership team, but I do so as a first among equals. My additional responsibilities give me particular tasks, in my view, but they do not make me more important. As a church family, we believe that the Holy Spirit resides within the body of the believers, and for that reason all major decisions that we make should involve all those who have made a commitment to be part of our local expression of the kingdom of God. That isn't always easy. What do I do when we as elders disagree about something? How do I, in the words of the Apostle Paul, make "every effort to maintain the unity of the Spirit in the bond of peace"?[65]

Presumably this work of maintaining unity is not easy – otherwise we would not have the encouragements of the New Testament to work at it quite so hard. Paul, writing to the Romans, seems to suggest that a united approach is not always possible, because at least two sides are present in any situation of conflict. He tells the Roman Christians:

> *If it is possible, so far as it depends on you, live peaceably with all.*
>
> Romans 12:18

Very few decisions made in a church with an ecclesiology like ours are unanimous. Occasionally they are, but not often. For example, when I was called to lead the church here the vote was 96 per cent. The decision was almost unanimous but not quite.[66] There have been other decisions where opinion has been much more divided. How do we protect unity in those moments as a local church?

How do I handle unity across the churches in our area?

As a leader of a local church that is part of the wider church in our geographic area, I also grapple with difficult conversations and issues. Where does our openness to dialogue and partnership with other churches start and where does it end? Can we participate in joint acts of worship with those of different denominations? What do we do with the reality that we are still barred from receiving bread and wine in a Roman Catholic service? How do we address issues of theological difference with other Christian churches in a way that protects unity but also stands for the truth? When I go to a local ministers' meeting, what do I say or do when issues such as the ones I deal with as pastor come up? How do I handle the Christians who come to our church from other fellowships with their stories of being mistreated or unhappy? Do I sent them back to their original church every time? Is it possible that some have been wrong to leave their own church and some, who have done all they can to address the issues that have concerned them, have done the right thing in leaving? How do I handle these situations with my fellow leaders?

How do I handle unity within the denomination of which my church is a part?

I am in an unusual position insofar as I have the privilege of leading a Baptist church but I am also an accredited minister with the Elim Pentecostal Church. As I write, I have just returned from the Elim Leaders' Summit which was held in the Harrogate International Centre. One of my colleagues has just returned from the Baptist Assembly, which was held in the same venue two days after the Elim Summit ended! Both denominations, rightly, have expectations of me. I am happy to conform to their demands and their expectations as much as I am able. It has not been an easy road for them to navigate what to do with someone like me. I am deeply committed to Elim, and count it a privilege and joy to sit under the leadership of that movement. In fact, as well as being the lead pastor of Gold Hill, the church I lead in Buckinghamshire, I am also one of the pastors of Kensington Temple in London, the largest Elim church in the United Kingdom. The latter is led by Colin Dye and I consider it an honour and a privilege to meet with him and to be accountable to him and to the national leadership team of the Elim Church. At the same time, however, I am committed to the local Baptist church that I lead. Most people at Gold Hill have little concern about the term "Baptist", and much prefer to define themselves as Christians. We rarely use the word "Baptist" in our publicity and our signage, but we are, nevertheless, part of that stream. I want to honour that and to honour the leaders of the Baptist Union of Great Britain.[67]

The last few years of leadership within the Baptist Union have been difficult for me. It has felt like my conservative, evangelical, charismatic stance has been endured by the Baptist Union rather than welcomed or celebrated. Decisions around tolerance, inclusion, and the autonomy of local churches have left me and many other leaders like me scratching our heads as we try to figure out how to respond to what feels like an increasing move toward liberalism in areas of personal ethics and the interpretation of Scripture. On more than one occasion our church leadership has wondered whether it is time to leave the Central Baptist Association, of which we are a part, and seek a new relationship with another association or, indeed, another church family. We have not done so. The reason is that we want to work out what it means to be part of a church movement that grapples with disagreements and listens to one another. We believe we need the challenges of the wider family of Baptist churches, and we also believe that we have something fundamentally important to say to the Baptist family. We are not passive about the contentious issues that the wider movement is grappling with; we are passionate about trying to persuade the wider Baptist Church to remain rooted in the DNA of our founding fathers and mothers. That is not an easy position to be in. It's hard to maintain unity in a context like this – but just because it is hard does not mean that it should be abandoned.

As an Elim minister, I grapple with the emphasis that classic Pentecostalism places on healing and the apparent failure to develop a theology of pain within the church stream. Our pietistic understanding of the Foursquare Gospel of Jesus as Saviour, Healer, Baptizer, and Coming King needs a radical re-examination as we enter the second century of Pentecostalism, and we need to remember that the Pentecostal outpouring of the early twentieth century was a gift to the whole church and not just the Pentecostal church.[68] Classic Pentecostalism needs to face the challenges of the exaggerated claims and over-realized eschatology of the Word of Faith movement if we are to avoid becoming perceived as a cult. How do we do that? Once again, I find myself in a position where it is hard to maintain unity – but just because it is hard does not mean that it should be abandoned.

How do I handle unity within my wider ministry?

I have been blessed and amazed at the privilege of serving God. He has allowed me to speak across denominations and streams across the world. I have seen His beauty and His grace at work in so many different church streams, denominations, and movements. No stream or denomination has everything right, but I have met remarkable men and women of faith in these denominations. From Roman Catholics with a deep love of Jesus Christ and a deep experience of His grace to members of new church movements such as The Vineyard or New Frontiers and pretty much everything in between, I have been deeply blessed and encouraged by the work of the Holy Spirit in the lives of His people.

Such a privileged position brings with it many responsibilities, however. How do I maintain unity in these various contexts? Five hundred years after Martin Luther nailed the ninety-five theses to the door of the University of Wittenberg, there are still many areas of disagreement and concern between those of us (and I include myself) in the Protestant streams of the church and those within the Roman Catholic tradition. The Joint Declaration on the Doctrine of Justification that was issued by the Lutheran World Federation and the Catholic Church[69] leaves significant questions still unanswered and is not, in my view, the end of the matter at all.[70] There are significant issues across denominations that have a deep impact on what it means to be faithful followers of Christ.

Learning to disagree without being disagreeable

Unity isn't easy – but it is important. So how do we do it? How do we learn to disagree without being disagreeable? Having previously explored that each individual Christian's self-understanding flows from who we are in Christ, this must surely also be the starting point for our unity as churches, but that is harder than it sounds.

Agreement on secondary issues is man's idea; unity in core convictions is God's idea[71]

Agreement on secondary issues is not the same as unity on core convictions. Agreement on secondary issues is only possible sometimes, but unity on core convictions is vital in the body of Christ if we are to live in the blessing of God's gift of unity to us. Only as we understand this will we be able to work out how to express our differences and our disagreements without fracturing. Agreement implies that we are aspiring to some level of uniformity, whereas unity allows for a sameness that is expressed through diversity. This doesn't mean that putting unity above agreement makes it easier, but it does make it clearer. Let me illustrate the point that I am trying to make by using one of my own experiences as an example.

When I came to lead Gold Hill in 2010, I recognized that I was stepping into the leadership of a church that had a strong reputation among the Christian community on the role of women in the church, and it was not one that I shared. Gold Hill's position was one that would be described as complementarianism.[72] At least two of my predecessors, David Pawson and Jim Graham, publicly held to this position. Indeed, David Pawson's book, *Leadership is*

Male, has had a strong impact in the Christian world,[73] and Jim's wife, Anne Graham, wrote a book about womanhood while at Gold Hill that expressed a strong complementarian view of the role of women.[74] My position on the role of women in the church is an egalitarian one.[75] One of the questions that I was asked as both the church and I considered whether it would be right for me to come and lead them was what I would do about this potential conflict. My response was simple: I would teach an egalitarian understanding of the Scriptures and ask the church to lift its ban on women holding the office of elder or pastor and the assumption that women should not preach or teach in the church.

During the first year of my leadership of the church we explored the issue together. I taught the eldership my position and answered their questions. I then taught the wider church family and gave them the opportunity to ask questions. We then had a six-month period for people to reflect and pray. The church meeting approved Gold Hill moving to a place of egalitarianism with a 74 per cent majority; we required a 66 per cent majority for the decision to be carried. Since then we have seen an increase in the affirmation of women in ministry. We have both male and female elders, we have both male and female pastors, and we have both male and female preachers. The church is increasingly embracing both men and women in the gifts that God has given them. Gold Hill is a stronger church because of this decision, and it is also a stronger church because of how the decision was made.

I did not set out to persuade the church to agree with me. Instead, in my teaching and explanation I made it clear that there is evidence in Scripture for the complementarian view. My point was that there is also clear evidence in the Scriptures for the egalitarian view. For all who were part of the church family, my aim was to help them see the biblical validity of an egalitarian view. If they still chose to believe in complementarianism then I would respect that.

There were a number of things that I asked them to assent to:

1. That the egalitarian view had biblical foundations too.

2. That a number of people in the church family might hold an egalitarian position.

3. That the church family were ultimately responsible for making a decision together about where we stood on the issue.

4. That egalitarians had accepted the established view of the church (complementarian) for many years and that what I was asking them to consider was whether this position needed to change. If the majority of the church believed it was time for us to move to an egalitarian view then we would simply be asking those whose view had once shaped the direction of the church to accept that they were part of a wider community where the egalitarian view would now shape the church. Both sides of the discussion would be free to affirm or not prospective elders according to their theological convictions. We would never impose our views on one another; we would respect one another.

5. As important as this decision was, it was not an issue of salvation.

6. As important as this decision was, it was not a vote of confidence in my leadership, and I committed to staying in my

role whether the church agreed with me or not. In the same spirit, I asked the church family to make a decision to remain part of the body whether they agreed with the decision or not. This was not an issue that needed to split the church. Instead, it was an opportunity to display our unity in the midst of potential disagreement.

I remember the night of the decision very clearly. When we announced the result, a cheer was raised by a few people in the room. I immediately asked that this be quietened and that we remember that for some in the room the decision was one that they would struggle to affirm. I believe that was the right thing to do. Around sixty people had voted against us moving to an egalitarian position, but around 180 had voted in favour of it. My responsibility was to pastor the whole church through this change. I made it clear that no one needed to leave Gold Hill over the issue, and I began the task of building a sense of common purpose in the gospel and in the mission of God rather than dwelling on the discussions around the role of women.

Of our membership (around 650 people), four people left as they felt unable to support the change. I miss them to this day, but I recognized that I could not force them to stay in a church that they felt had made a fundamentally wrong decision. Of those who disagreed with the decision, the rest remained part of our church. Many of them have now changed their position as they have seen women ministering and have experienced personally the blessing of their ministry. Some, however, remain in a place where they find it difficult to relate to a woman preaching, or where they would prefer to talk through an issue of governance or leadership with a man. A number would struggle to see a woman appointed as the senior leader of a church. We accept these concerns. We accept that some will choose not to attend a service when a woman is preaching. We do not condemn them for it, and they do not condemn the church for the position we now hold. Instead, we are united in our common cause for Christ. We have allowed this issue to sit in a secondary place and not in a primary one. As a result, the church is stronger than it has ever been.

An interesting spin-off of this issue for us was that two of the three previous senior pastors remained in Gold Hill when I came to lead the church. Steve Gaukroger is still part of our congregational life, and Jim Graham remained a solid supporter of the church until his death in July 2016. Both of these men, while disagreeing with my position, conducted themselves with the utmost grace and kindness. Jim and I were open about our differences, but we never allowed them to become points of division. On a number of occasions we shared our differences of opinion on the issue, and the impact on the audiences to which we were ministering was profound. Jim and Anne remained close personal friends until their deaths and both happily received ministry from both men and women. Steve and Jan Gaukroger have never made this an issue in our friendship or in our partnership in the gospel.

This approach is what I mean by the reality that we do not have to agree with one another in order to be united. Of course, the issue of the role of women is a secondary issue, not a primary one. Agreement on secondary issues is not vital for biblical unity.

Common conviction in the fundamentals is absolutely essential

Common convictions on the fundamentals of our faith are absolutely vital to biblical unity. I am not sure that it is possible to remain in close fellowship and partnership if our disagreements are of a primary nature. In fact, the New Testament is littered with examples of strong invective and passionate language when it comes to issues of primary concern. When it came to points of view that could lead people away from the gospel of the Lord Jesus Christ, the leaders of the early church were crystal clear in their warnings and their actions.

Paul warned the Galatian Christians not to desert the One who had called them to live in the grace of the Lord Jesus, and he chastised them for allowing a different gospel to take hold of their hearts, which he described as no gospel at all:

> I am astonished that you are so quickly deserting the one who called you in the grace of Christ and are turning to a different gospel – not that there is another gospel, but there are some who are confusing you and want to pervert the gospel of Christ. But even if we or an angel from heaven should proclaim to you a gospel contrary to what we proclaimed to you, let that one be accursed! As we have said before, so now I repeat, if anyone proclaims to you a gospel contrary to what you received, let that one be accursed!
>
> Am I now seeking human approval, or God's approval? Or am I trying to please people? If I were still pleasing people, I would not be a servant of Christ.
>
> Galatians 1:6–10

He even suggests that those who are perpetuating this wrong understanding of the gospel should circumcise themselves:

I wish those who unsettle you would castrate themselves!

Galatians 5:12

Paul's warning to the Philippians was just as strong.[76] It would be true to say that the New Testament is littered with strong warnings to those who depart from core convictions about the gospel.[77] John the Baptist calls his opponents a "brood of vipers",[78] and Jesus uses exactly the same language of the same people, adding that they are like "whitewashed tombs" and "blind fools".[79] He tells the religious leaders who oppose Him that they belong to their father, the devil.[80] And even His closest followers are rebuked strongly; after all, He used a metaphor to describe Peter as Satan himself.[81]

So perhaps it is fair to say that our definition of what is acceptable language in disagreement and the definition of what the Scriptures would see as acceptable disagreement are not exactly the same thing! What is clear is that when it comes to the truth of the gospel, what we believe really matters.

> *Gospel truth matters and is a blessing to the world, so should be defended against errors that obscure the Gospel and can be seriously detrimental for people's spiritual health. Error is dangerous and needs to be strenuously resisted and named for what it is – a powerful force that opposes the God of truth and threatens to damage the life and mission of the Church.*[82]

We, as followers of Jesus, must not court controversy, but we must not shy away from it if we encounter it because we are standing for the deep truth of the gospel. In the words of John Stott:

There is something wrong with us if we relish controversy...
Controversy conducted in a hostile way, which descends to
personal insult and abuse, stains all too many of the pages
of church history. But we cannot avoid controversy itself.
"Defending and confirming the Gospel" [Philippians 1:7] is
part of what God calls us to do.[83]

What are primary issues and what are secondary issues?

If disagreeing without being disagreeable is at least partly dependent upon identifying what are primary and secondary issues, then we need to know how to identify what is a primary issue and what is a secondary one. If there are issues upon which we must stand firm, and there are others that are of secondary consequence, then the most important question for us to consider must be which is which.

I would suggest a simple metric for this, although this may not be enough for many Christians. I would want to go back to the great creedal confessions of the Christian church and allow these to be the fundamentals around which we gather.[84]

I sit within the evangelical part of the church, and for many of my fellow evangelicals the central expressions of our faith might be the Evangelical Alliance statement of faith.[85] While I treasure this expression of faith dearly and hold to it, I am not sure that it can be the basis around which broader Christian unity can be successfully enabled. The same could be said for me for the Elim statement of faith,[86] or the Baptist Declaration of Principle.[87] These statements, along with many others, are expressions of deep conviction around which many Christians can gather, including me. They can form strong and positive rallying points for particular aspects of the body of Christ in a nation or in the world. I readily and gladly identify with people in these parts of Christ's family around the world, and there are many situations in which these would be the centre of our reflections together. I embrace their expressions, celebrate the commonality that they bring, and cherish the opportunities that come from connecting with and ministering alongside people who hold the same principles and priorities as I do. It may even be that these are the benchmark for some aspects of our expressions of unity and mutual commitment, but they are not enough to unite the body of Christ more widely. I embrace these just as I would embrace the Westminster Catechism,[88] the Heidelberg Catechism,[89] and the Augsburg Confession,[90] but each of these articulates a particular perspective[91] of the Christian church which does not include, for me, a broad enough scope of the expression of unity that is enabled through the prayer of Jesus in John 17 or the great declaration of Paul in Ephesians 4. Just as I could not ascribe to the 39 articles of the Anglican Church,[92] I accept that other fellow believers would not be able to ascribe to the specific doctrinal statements I have cited.

Common soil

It could be argued that it is only in the great creedal confessions of the church that we discover the common soil from which we all flourish. The three great confessions of the church are commonly understood to be the Apostles' Creed,[93] the Nicene Creed,[94] and the Chalcedonian Declaration.[95] Within these confessions we find the heartbeat of Christian conviction, fashioned over the first few centuries of the church. I am not sure that they say all that needs to be said – there is little in them about the life of Jesus other than the moments of His birth, His death, His resurrection, and His return, for example. There is little in them of the missional call of the church and the command to make disciples. We will find few words in them about the authority of the Scriptures. They speak little of the nature of baptism, and one could argue that the role of the Holy Spirit is not explained sufficiently. Many of these aspects of Christian expression have become increasingly important to us as we have progressed. I celebrate these doctrinal distinctives, but not at the expense of the core convictions that hold the entire church together. It is in the creeds that we find these expressions.

If we want to keep our Baptist churches together, then of course we explore the Baptist Declaration of Principle. If we want to keep our Elim churches together, then of course we explore the Elim of statement of faith, and so on. If we want to unite as evangelicals, then of course we stand around a common statement such as that of the Evangelical Alliance. All of these expressions of unity are helpful and inspiring. There is a greater unity, however, that we must each strive to protect. I am not talking about a bland expression of ecumenism that avoids saying anything difficult so that we can stay together, but rather a passionate unity grounded in what we, as Christians, believe about God, His work in the world, and His call upon the church.

The ultimate purpose of this unity is not only that we, those who are already Christians, might enjoy it, but rather that the world might believe that the Father has sent the Son.[96] In the words of the former Archbishop of Canterbury, George Carey:

The ultimate reconciliation that should concern us all is for the world to be reconciled with its Maker. Thus, ecumenism is about liberating the Church to get on with the task of mission. It is about being a credible instrument, a prophetic sign and an eschatological foretaste of the healing of Christ. So yes, it does matter that Churches are in unreconciled diversity because how we lie contradicts the message we proclaim, the full, visible unity of God's Church is then an urgent missionary imperative, not just something to fulfil Church politics.[97]

Ecumenism for its own sake does not automatically lead to life. Protecting the unity that is given to us in Christ not only leads to life and hope within the church, but it also leads to that life flowing to the communities around us. Such unity leads to new life in the experience of not-yet-Christians as they come to a knowledge of the love of God in Christ, shown to and through the church. There is too much at stake for us to settle for a bland, lifeless, and directionless unity, and there is too much at stake for us to say that unity doesn't matter.

As Christians in a town, a country, a nation, or the world, if we want to find a way of standing together and celebrating our common life and our common cause, then it is to the creeds that we turn. They are, at least in some way, the starting point of our common expression of life together and faith in Christ. I list them here, without further comment, as the theological foundations of our unity, before beginning to explore ways in which we might strengthen our expressions of unity relationally. If we are to build a strong, lasting and effective unity in our communities, our nation, or our world, I can think of no better place to start than here.[98]

Apostles Creed[99]

I believe in God, the Father almighty,
Creator of heaven and earth.

I believe in Jesus Christ, his only Son, our Lord.
He was conceived by the power of the Holy Spirit
and born of the Virgin Mary.

He suffered under Pontius Pilate,
was crucified, died, and was buried.

He descended to the dead.
On the third day he rose again.
He ascended into heaven,
and is seated at the right hand of the Father.
He will come again to judge the living and the dead.

I believe in the Holy Spirit,
the holy catholic Church,
the communion of saints,
the forgiveness of sins,
the resurrection of the body,
and the life everlasting.

Amen.

The Nicene Creed[100]

We believe in one God,
the Father, the Almighty,
maker of heaven and earth,
of all that is, seen and unseen.

We believe in one Lord, Jesus Christ,
the only Son of God,
eternally begotten of the Father,
God from God, Light from Light,
true God from true God,
begotten, not made,
of one Being with the Father.
Through him all things were made.

For us and for our salvation
he came down from heaven:
by the power of the Holy Spirit
he became incarnate from the Virgin Mary,
and was made man.

For our sake he was crucified under Pontius Pilate;
he suffered death and was buried.
On the third day he rose again
in accordance with the Scriptures;
he ascended into heaven
and is seated at the right hand of the Father.

He will come again in glory to judge the living and the dead,
and his kingdom will have no end.

We believe in the Holy Spirit, the Lord, the giver of life,
who proceeds from the Father and the Son.

With the Father and the Son he is worshiped and glorified.
He has spoken through the Prophets.
We believe in one holy catholic and apostolic Church.
We acknowledge one baptism for the forgiveness of sins.
We look for the resurrection of the dead,
and the life of the world to come.

Amen.

The Chalcedonian Declaration[101]

Therefore, following the holy fathers, we all with one accord
       teach men to acknowledge
one and the same Son, our Lord Jesus Christ,
at once complete in Godhead and complete in manhood,
truly God and truly man,
consisting also of a reasonable soul and body;
of one substance with the Father as regards his Godhead,
and at the same time of one substance with us as regards his
       manhood;
like us in all respects, apart from sin;
as regards his Godhead, begotten of the Father before the
       ages,
but yet as regards his manhood begotten, for us men and for
       our salvation, of Mary the Virgin, the Godbearer;
one and the same Christ, Son, Lord, Only-begotten,
recognized in two natures, without confusion, without
       change, without division, without separation;
the distinction of natures being in no way annulled by the
       union,
but rather the characteristics of each nature being preserved
and coming together to form one person and subsistence,
not as parted or separated into two persons,
but one and the same Son and Only-begotten God the Word,
       Lord Jesus Christ;
even as the prophets from earliest times spoke of him, and our
       Lord Jesus Christ himself taught us,
and the creed of the fathers has handed down to us.

Toward a Code of Conduct

One of the hardest things to do is to make a commitment to consistently tell the truth to someone else. It demands an ongoing willingness to bind ourselves to grace, to truth, and to love. It demands that we embrace grace, because without it we will sound aloof and judgmental or self-abased and dejected. It demands our commitment to the truth, because without truth our relationships have no foundation. It demands consistent willingness to love, because without love, all of our other actions and intentions amount to nothing. In the words of the Apostle Paul, if we do not love, we are nothing.[102]

A lesson from marriage

In their book on marriage, Tim and Kathy Keller make the point that grace, truth, and love are key ingredients in a sustainable and healthy marriage.[103] At its heart, marriage is not a contractual relationship, but rather a covenantal one in which a man and a woman make promises to one another that are binding and sacrificial commitments to seek the good of the other person.

In many ways, there are lessons to be learned from marriage for protecting unity between Christians. Learning to trust one another, to love one another, and to share life together are vital components of a healthy marriage, and they are essential components of healthy relationships between Christians. Just think how different the relationships between Christians would be if we sought after the principles of love as set out in Paul's great description of love:

> *Love is patient; love is kind; love is not envious or boastful or arrogant or rude. It does not insist on its own way; it is not irritable or resentful; it does not rejoice in wrongdoing, but rejoices in the truth. It bears all things, believes all things, hopes all things, endures all things.*
>
> 1 Corinthians 13:4–7

Marriages involve navigating differences of opinion and points of view – as do relationships between Christians. Marriages involve being willing to listen more than we talk if we want our relationships to be strong – as do relationships between Christians. Marriages involve a commitment to do everything we can to stay together and to work through issues of conflict until we reach a solution – as do relationships between Christians. Marriages sometimes fail, and when they do, there are always deep hurts on both sides, lessons to be learned, and principles to put in place as the people involved move forward. The same is true for Christian relationships. The Apostle Paul reminded the believers in Ephesus that relationships between them took time and effort:

> *We must no longer be children, tossed to and fro and blown about by every wind of doctrine, by people's trickery, by their craftiness in deceitful scheming. But speaking the truth in*

love, we must grow up in every way into him who is the head, into Christ, from whom the whole body, joined and knitted together by every ligament with which it is equipped, as each part is working properly, promotes the body's growth in building itself up in love.

Ephesians 4:14–16

Before my wife and I were married we asked our pastor if we could have some marriage preparation classes. Our church was not really used to running that kind of thing, so we ended up with one session in which we talked about a range of issues. It helped a little, but not as much as we would have liked. So we decided that we would prepare for our married life by reading some books together about the challenges and the blessings of marriage. We discussed issues such as how we would address conflict, what our key priorities were as individuals and as a couple, how we would handle money, what we sensed we wanted to do with our lives, what we felt were one another's callings, and how we could disciple one another. We made commitments around praying together, worshipping together, investing in our relationship, listening to one another, and studying the Scriptures together. We discussed our ideas and thoughts about when to have children and the way we felt we should bring them up. We explored the baggage that each of us brought to the marriage. Some of that baggage was important and good, such as good lessons from our parents, from other relationships, and from other marriages that we had been able to see into. Some of that baggage, however, was not so good, such as mistakes we had made or mistakes we had witnessed in others. We wanted to do everything we could to make sure our relationship was strong and that we would continually invest in it. We were married in 1993 and we are still investing in our marriage. We are still making mistakes. We still learn new things about one another. We still hurt one another. We still have to forgive one another. We are still growing in our trust of one another and in our commitments to one another.

How can we do the same thing in our relationships as Christians? How can we strengthen our relationships within our own church families as well as our relationships across local churches? Are there ways in which we can put some guidelines in place so that when we do enter periods of conflict we have a set of agreed principles to help us? There is a certain level of inevitability about the fact that we hurt one another. We say the wrong thing. We take something that someone else says to us the wrong way. We hurt one another. The inevitability of our errors does not, however, need to be matched with complacency and ambivalence. We can find ways of investing in our relationships with other Christians in our local church and with other churches in our local area. We can make it a priority to love one another; after all, this in and of itself has a dramatic impact on the world around us. The Lord Jesus reminded His followers of this principle when He told them that the world would know that they were His disciples by their love for one another:

> *I give you a new commandment, that you love one another. Just as I have loved you, you also should love one another. By this everyone will know that you are my disciples, if you have love for one another.*
>
> John 13:34–35

We are a family,[104] and as a family we can find ways of loving one another and honouring one another. As a family we can also find ways of being honest with one another about our disagreements without pretending they are not there. Family gatherings where everyone is being polite and no one is being honest are unbearable for all concerned. On the other hand, family gatherings where everyone spends the whole time squabbling and fighting are also unbearable. My best memories of family are the times when we were together and we knew we were different, but we still loved one another. We listened to one another. We respected one another. That is what family is supposed to do. So how do we, as Christians, behave more like a family and less like a society or a club? We start by allowing the metaphor of being a family to shape the way we see one another. In our hallway at home we have a poster that says the following:

In this family...
We do real
We do really loud
We do mistakes
We do hugs
We do forgiveness
We do I'm sorry
We do second chances
We do believing
We do praying
We do God's Word
We do family
We do love.

That is not a bad place to start. In our local churches, as we live out our faith side by side, we could make loving one another a higher commitment than always having to agree with one another. As I have already suggested, agreement on secondary issues is a human idea; unity is God's idea. What would it look like for our church communities to agree a common code of conduct? Why couldn't our churches have a charter to which we would commit that outlines the way we would handle disagreements?

Laying good foundations – churches together local covenants[105]

A commitment to shared values and behaviours can go a long way to helping local churches work together more effectively. Setting out together how you intend to behave before you face conflict or disagreement is much better than having to work it out when you are in the middle of a difference of opinion. Agreeing how we will behave is a good way of making sure that we also hold one another accountable for our life together.

Before going any further, though, I would want to argue that unity for the sake of unity will be of little use to anyone. Unity is not "at any cost". There are significant issues between local churches and national/global denominations that cannot be ignored if we are to build a better unity. We cannot pretend that issues do not matter. Subjects such as the priesthood, our understanding of the sacraments, the way we make decisions, the nature of initiation into the Christian community, the place or validity of conversion, and the roles of grace and works are just a few of the subjects that churches can find difficult to discuss, precisely because we do not agree on them. When local church partnerships refuse to discuss these issues and others like them for the sake of unity, it can feel like one of the family gatherings I was talking about earlier, where everyone feels very uncomfortable. Healthy local cross-church groups will not be afraid to address these issues. Some of them will be unresolvable; others can be resolved. Some will lead to uncomfortable discussions about what we can and we cannot do together. Let me give you an example.

I am deeply indebted to the local church leaders where I live for their love, support, and encouragement. I am grateful for the unity and the love that we share. In fact, my first book on unity was dedicated to a dear friend who is a beautiful Christian and a Roman Catholic. Others in the group are Anglicans. Some are Methodists. One or two are Baptists. When we meet, we meet as Christians, and we unite around the love and the grace of God shown to us through the Lord Jesus Christ, but there are still major areas of disagreement between us, and they still matter. I cannot partake in Holy Communion at the Roman Catholic Church, which is located a few hundred yards from where I live. In fact, even if I could do so by invitation I would be unable to do so out of conviction. I have a fundamentally different understanding of what happens in Communion to those in the Roman Catholic Church. I could not, with a clear conscience, take part in a Mass. I have theological convictions about it that would prevent me from doing so. Furthermore, as I said in the previous chapter, despite discussions over the years, including the dialogue between the Lutherans and the Roman Catholics at the end of the 1990s around justification,[106] there are still major issues to discuss and address. The issue of salvation by grace through faith is still a very important one.

On another front, a young man in my congregation is getting married in 2018. He comes from a Baptist church and his fiancée comes from an Anglican church. They really wanted me to marry them in his fiancée's church, but the vicar there will not permit it. The reason is that I am not allowed to conduct a wedding in the Anglican church.

In many gatherings I attend across the country, an Anglican vicar has to preside at Communion otherwise the service has to be called a sharing service because, for some, Communion must have a prescribed form and set of words.

I am not trying to lay out a list of preferences for you to pick and choose from! Rather, my point is that there are still very important differences between churches. We do not serve the cause of unity either by pretending they are not there or by pretending that they do not matter. They are there and they do matter.[107]

I am not sure that current models of ecumenism always strike the right balance when it comes to unity, because so often ecumenism avoids these issues or makes them into interesting topics of conversation. It would be better to allow honest, even if heated and passionate, discussion about them while at the same time being clear about what does unite us. I am convinced that if we are to protect our unity and build our sense of common purpose, we must be willing and able to discuss the issues that we agree on – but we must also discuss the issues on which we do not agree. It is as we seek to define and strengthen our unity that we can also acknowledge its limits. To fail to do so will only exclude those who are suspicious of it in the first place.

Having acknowledged the complexities of our unit, however, I am convinced that there are really good lessons to learn from local churches that are trying to work out how to stand shoulder to shoulder with one another.[108]

A covenant between local churches can help to set the parameters of the relationship that different congregations can enjoy. It can be formal or informal. Such covenants come in many forms and can be the basis of a variety of ways of experiencing Christian community together.[109] As local churches consider how they can stand alongside one another, there are important questions to explore, such as:

1. What is it that unites you? What will be the basis of your expression of unity?

2. What do you have a vision of doing together instead of doing separately?

3. How does your local expression of unity relate to the wider community in your geographic area, and how does your Christian unity relate to the church around the world?

4. What will be the additional benefits of this expression of unity? What will it achieve?

5. What will it look like in the day-to-day life of your local community and the day-to-day lives of the churches?[110]

6. What are the areas where there are differences and how will you address them? Can they all be addressed or do some simply need to be acknowledged rather than resolved?

7. Are there limits to your expression of unity? What things are you unable to do together?

As local churches explore this kind of commitment to unity, there are other important issues to consider. For example, does your unity need to be formal or can it be informal? If you are in a small geographic area, should the local congregations combine so that the witness can be stronger and is more sustainable? How long will the partnership or the agreement last, and who will be the main contributors? The last question is an important one, given the reality that leaders of churches come and go too. The best forms of local unity do not simply exist at the level of the leaders of the local churches, but they also exist in the hearts of local congregations. It is not unusual for local churches to work well together when specific leaders are committed to one another and then for that unity to dissolve when a leader leaves. This happens because the unity was only at the superficial level of the leaders and did not knit together the hearts of the Christians in a community. For expressions of unity to last, they need to involve as many people as possible at as many levels as possible.

If we can establish a good understanding of our attitudes toward one another, we will be much more prepared when things go wrong. Just like marriage preparation helps a couple to address their relationship strengths, weaknesses, and pressure points before they are forced to, so local church covenants help local churches to do the same. A good example of this is the Churches Together Group in Hitchin.[111] This local expression of Christian unity includes eighteen local churches and involves them working together, serving together, praying together, and speaking well of one another. The ministers from the local churches meet together regularly, and in addition each church has up to four other representatives who meet to plan how they can serve together.

They think about projects for which they can pool resources and ways in which they can stand together as a witness to Christ in the local community.

Local churches can also join together in local mission partnerships or mission unity movements.[112] An example of such an approach is Gather.[113] This national network of vibrant missional unity movements in villages, towns, and cities across the UK is linked to a global family of mission movements that are putting mission at the heart of unity.

Churches working together in mission release more energy, enthusiasm, and enterprise than would be released if churches were to work alone. From Christ First in Middlesbrough[114] to Bath Churches Together and Bath Christian Action Network (BathCAN),[115] local churches are working together to create a better witness in the communities around them and to the world.

Gweini is the Council of the Christian Voluntary Sector in Wales and another example of mission-focused partnership and unity. It was established in 1999 by a partnership between Care for the Family, Cornerstone Church Swansea, the Evangelical Alliance for Wales, and Tearfund. It seeks to serve the Christian Voluntary Sector in Wales through representation, networking, and sharing information.[116]

The Association of Related Churches in Ireland (ARC)[117] helps plant new churches across Ireland, both Northern and Southern. Its team of church leaders and planters from both sides of the border help those interested in unity and mission to discover how they can work together and extend the kingdom of God. ARC wants to strengthen existing churches by creating a community of leaders with a heart to reach the nation together. It wants to create a space for resources to be shared and to see a community of Christian leaders committed to one another relationally and to the wider community in mission. At the heart of who it is and what it does, ARC is seeking to be centred on Christ, spiritually healthy, strategically growing, culturally attractive, and to have a focus on mission.

There are hundreds of expressions of healthy Christian unity across the United Kingdom, where local churches have found that they are stronger when they work together and serve together. These expressions of unity lay a foundation for better dialogue when challenges arise and disagreements threaten to fracture the witness of the church in a local community. Yet the fact still remains that a charter for conduct when opposition does happen would be an extremely helpful tool.

A code of conduct for a local church seeking to work with other churches

I believe it is possible to set out a few basic principles whereby a local church or local churches can develop an agreed code of conduct that protects the unity of the body of Christ while at the same time avoiding the pitfalls of unity for the sake of unity. Such a code of conduct is not easy, but it is possible. It will involve difficult decisions and hard conversations, but these will strengthen the expression of Christian unity in a local area.

1. We are committed to a common declaration of Christian faith[118] and will not allow issues of secondary importance to create division. We recognize as brothers and sisters all those whom God has brought into His family.

2. We will, at all times, seek to have the mind and attitude of Christ toward other people, and we will seek to protect the unity of the Spirit in the bond of peace by speaking well of one another, believing the best of one another, and seeking to resolve conflicts in a dignified, gracious, and Christlike way.

3. We are committed to biblical principles of relationship which include avoiding public arguments and disagreements as much as possible, listening carefully to one another, speaking the truth in love, and ensuring that we employ the stages of conflict resolution set out in Matthew 18:15–20.

4. Recognizing the instructions of the Apostle Paul in 1 Corinthians 6, we will seek to avoid bringing conflicts to a court of law wherever possible.

5. We will put the witness of the church, the Lordship of Christ, and faithfulness to the gospel above any other commitment, including the reputations of our own denominations or local churches or our personal popularity.

6. We will be clear about what we can do together, seeking to maximize the potential for our common life, and we will be clear about what we cannot do together, seeking to minimize those things.

7. We will hold the tension of grace, truth, and love together at all times and as much as is humanly possible.

8. There will be times when working together is no longer possible because of deep disagreements in ecclesial practice,

theology, pastoral perspective, or mission. In such situations, we will seek to respect and honour one another, even if we cannot agree, and we will do everything we can to keep talking and keep seeking ways of standing together and understanding one another.

9. Division will always be a last resort and, we pray, a temporary state until such time as our conflict can be resolved and we can celebrate our common faith and mission again.

10. We will pray for one another and love one another always.

I have employed these principles for many years as a leadership consultant for churches and Christian charities. Time and time again I have discovered that if we can only learn to listen more than we speak and learn to see others through the eyes of Christ, then we would fracture much less. I offer these principles humbly, recognizing that I myself have broken them. I have seen churches in a local town turn their backs on one another so many times. They have sometimes separated over issues that were genuinely important, such as the message of the gospel, the importance of mission, the centrality of Christ, the identity of God, the meaning of salvation, or the authority of the Bible. Yet sometimes they have fractured because leaders could not cope with another church's success, or because one congregation was growing at the expense of another and no one did anything about it, or because of insecurity, old divisions, or resentment. I wish it were not so. No matter how godly the leader or how focused the stream, we all make mistakes.[119] Think of the arguments that could be avoided, the heartbreak that could be healed, and the situations that could be resolved between churches in local communities if we were to employ the principles set out in this simple code of conduct. I am not claiming that it is perfect, but I am suggesting it could help many local churches to find one another again.

As I progress in leadership I am learning that God has a great deal to do in me. Some years ago, as a young pastor, I had a very long list of things that were essential to me. At the more frivolous end that list included the clothes that someone could wear, the version of the Bible that someone should read, the style of music that a public meeting should employ, and what Christians should do, or not do, on a Sunday. At the more serious end the list included the roles of men and women, the nature of church government, the way in which a Christian should be baptized, the nature of judgment, the centrality of preaching, the nature of the gifts of the Holy Spirit, and the best way to pray. At times my spiritual preferences became my dogma. Unless you agreed with me, you were wrong. I remember using phrases such as "the Bible clearly states" an awful lot. I look back on some of the ways I have conducted myself over the years with a deep sense of thankfulness for the grace of God and a deep sense of embarrassment at the ways I allowed my views to be so emphatically unchangeable.

I have had the privilege and the responsibility of pastoring in a number of churches. In each, God used me to do some good. In each, I think I made good decisions and helped people to grow in Christ. In each, I think I helped the church I served to connect with other churches in the community and in the nation. It would also be true to say, however, that in each I also argued about the wrong things sometimes. My list of non-negotiables was too long. I have allowed my preferences to be forced on people too often, and I have been too slow to listen and too fast to interrupt. These are traits that the Lord is still working on in me.

That having been said, there are key things that are still absolutely essential to me as a follower of Jesus. Without them, I struggle to understand how anyone can describe themselves as a Christian. They can be summed up, as we saw in an earlier chapter, in the great creeds of the church. I hold them more deeply now than I have ever held them. I am learning what it means to be a better pastor by learning what it means to hold unity more highly. I am learning to be more humble and to be open to the possibility that I might be wrong about more things than I care to admit and that others might be right. The blessing of faith is the ability to give other people the benefit of the doubt wherever possible. That is not to minimize truth; rather it is to hold truth and grace and love together in a powerful cord of conviction called Christian unity.

> *Whenever equally biblical Christians who are equally anxious to understand the reading of scripture and to submit to its authority reach different conclusions, we should deduce that evidently scripture is not crystal clear on this matter and therefore we can afford to give one another liberty. You can also hope – through prayer, study and discussion… to grow in understanding and so in… agreement.*[120]

The reality is that a fractured world needs a church that is united in mission and in its understanding of God. Our communities need to see that when we preach to them about reconciliation, we are willing to practise it ourselves. The people around us need to know that the community they are joining is one that is able to hold them, welcome them, love them, and make room for them. They need to know that we think they matter. They also need to know that we will tell them the truth and that we will not shrink away from the awkward and difficult things that love has to say sometimes. Above all, they need to know that we love them and that we love God. Loving them without loving God is not enough because they need more than our love to see their lives transformed and hope birthed. Loving God but not loving them is not enough either because they will feel like pew fodder, notches on our spiritual belt that are only temporarily important to us. They need us to love them and to love God because we are the conduits through which God will pour His love upon them, and they are conduits through whom God encounters us.

South Buckinghamshire needs all the churches that we have and more. With our varied worship styles, buildings, liturgies, social demographics, political standpoints, and geographic locations we each have a vital role to play in seeing our communities transformed and Christ exalted. We each play a small part in God's great plan. South Buckinghamshire also needs us to be one church, though. It needs to know that we love God and love one another. If we don't love one another, how will those in the locality ever believe that we genuinely love them? The people around us see people giving up on one another all the time. They see it in work, at home, and in college. Many of them have been victims of that abandonment; some have been the perpetrators of it. They need to see a church across the community that is alive, hopeful, loving, and united.

What is true in our area is true across the United Kingdom and across the world. A divided church cannot reach a fractured world. We need each other in our local communities across the streams and the denominations. We are stronger together.

Liberty not Licence

odern applications of the notions of tolerance and inclusion are decimating the reality of biblical unity because they are creating cultures that are in direct opposition to the terms being used. Champions of tolerance often end up sounding like the most intolerant people of all because any opinion that challenges theirs is wrong, while those who proclaim that the virtue of inclusion is paramount often do so while excluding the views of those who disagree with them. How do we protect a unity that makes room for one another while also allowing for robust disagreement? The words of the Apostle Paul might help us.

Addressing one another as brothers and sisters

It doesn't take a mastermind to see how important unity was in the New Testament. Paul talked about it a lot. He urged believers to worship together whether they were from a Jewish or a Gentile background,[121] and he reminded the believers in Galatia that they were united primarily because of Jesus, before anything else. Their gender, their social and economic status, and their cultural shaping were all secondary.[122] He told the believers in Galatia to hold on to the reality that they shared a father in Abraham.[123]

I am reminded of the vital importance of unity to the Apostle Paul by the simple fact that despite the various differences that he addressed in his letters, he consistently reminded them that they were also his brothers and sisters.[124] It could be argued that the church in Corinth was one of the most troublesome and fractured in his audience, yet he wrote to them with a deep sense of connectedness:

> *Paul, called to be an apostle of Christ Jesus by the will of God, and our brother Sosthenes, To the church of God that is in Corinth, to those who are sanctified in Christ Jesus, called to be saints, together with all those who in every place call on the name of our Lord Jesus Christ, both their Lord and ours: Grace to you and peace from God our Father and the Lord Jesus Christ.*
>
> 1 Corinthians 1:1–3

> *Paul, an apostle of Christ Jesus by the will of God, and Timothy our brother, To the church of God that is in Corinth, including all the saints throughout Achaia: Grace to you and peace from God our Father and the Lord Jesus Christ.*
>
> 2 Corinthians 1:1–2

It would appear that Paul was determined to have discussions with his opponents and critics as part of the Christian family, even when his rhetoric was strong and his language was severe.[125] Paul did not want threats from opponents to destroy the unity of the church,[126] but he was clear that what bound these believers together was their common allegiance to Jesus Christ.[127] They were to love each other with the humble, determined, and beautiful mind and example of the Lord Jesus at the centre of their thinking and as the clearest of their examples.[128]

Adiaphora[129] – understanding the difference between disputable matters and essentials[130]

By taking Paul's instructions to the churches in Corinth and Rome as our examples, we can discover how Paul helps the church to navigate its course between being absorbed by the culture of the day or by the legalism of the believing community. His guidance makes for a fascinating critique of the priorities of those communities and gives us invaluable insight into how to navigate troublesome straits for us.[131] Paul urged the Corinthian believers to avoid personality cults, to refrain from taking one another to court, and to live faithfully in a pagan culture. They were to come to the Lord's table united, and they were to remember they were one body when it came to the use of their gifts, the exercise of their ministries, and their participation in the life of the body of Jesus.[132] Paul's first letter to the Corinthians, it could be said, is all about unity.

What is interesting, however, is the way Paul tackled the issues at hand. Whereas many today would argue that we should forget about differences and just allow love, inclusion, and tolerance to shape the way we treat one another, Paul went further. He didn't dismiss difference; rather he redefined what really mattered and what really didn't. A cursory reading of Romans 14 and 15, for example, might suggest that Paul's guidance on eating meat sacrificed to idols and on observation of holy days means that what matters is our faith and that our practices are at best unimportant and at worst irrelevant. That would not, however, be an entirely accurate reading of the text. A closer examination actually gives us a way of understanding the challenges of unity for the Roman Christians and, by so doing, provides a possible way forward for us.

It is true to say that Paul outlined issues of primary and secondary importance for the believers in Rome and in Corinth. It is also true to say that he placed the eating of meat offered to idols and the observance of holy days as secondary in his writing. It is wrong, however, to assume that what he was actually saying was that behaviour and choices are secondary and that faith and grace are paramount. It is also wrong to assume that the modern equivalents of eating meat offered to idols and observing holy days are issues such as sexual ethics and marriage. Paul did not place sexual behaviour in a secondary category at any point in any of his letters. He did not make them issues of salvation, but he did demonstrate that our approach to them reflects what we understand about the impact of salvation in our lives. This matters in our culture because more and more Christians seem to be suggesting that issues of sexual morality and beliefs around marriage are negotiable, that it doesn't matter what we think about these topics, and that all of the perspectives can be right at the same time.[133] The implication could be that behaviour is simply a choice and that what really matters is conviction. In other words, if we think a behaviour is culturally and socially acceptable then it should be culturally and socially acceptable within the church. It doesn't actually matter whether the behaviour is sexual, ethical, economic, or relational. The argument would be that if a behaviour is seen as secondary, then whether we engage in it or not doesn't matter. That is true – but Paul moves beyond the definitions of "primary" or "secondary" being rooted in "faith" or "law" and gives us a new way of thinking. He helps us reconstruct the way we look at what is right or what is wrong through the lens of Jesus as our Messiah and the implications of His coming on both what we believe and how we behave.

Paul was consistently concerned about Christian behaviour in Rome and in Corinth. In Romans 1 and 2 he outlined behaviours that made people appear less than they were as they put their will and their ethics above God's, then he reversed the impact of the devastating assertion of our own way over God's way in Romans 12 and 13 as he described a better, more liberated, and deeply humanly dignifying way. Between chapters 6 and 8 of Romans he tackled sin and sinful behaviour head on, recognizing the struggle to do what was right and live well as one that was being raged within his own decisions, actions, and habits. He gives us hope while being honest about the challenges of our choices. The only way to be truly human and to be truly free is, according to Paul, to have our minds renewed.[134]

In Galatians, Paul is clear about behavioural expectations, setting out a list of the deeds of the flesh and the fruit of the Spirit clearly in chapter 5. Not only that, but Paul also warned his audience of the danger of living like the pagans do in other his other letters.[135] Paul never placed the choice between holiness and unity before the believers he was writing to. Holiness and unity are not mutually exclusive, and there is no need to choose one or the other. For Paul, unity was a primary issue and holiness was a primary evidence of the work of the Spirit in the life of the Christian. Paul was clear about that throughout his writing and ministry. We don't have to choose between unity and faithfulness to God any more than we have to choose between breath and breathing. One is deeply connected to other.

There is no greater threat to the unity of the church today than how we handle primary and secondary issues. On secondary issues, we should allow for freedom, difference, debate, discussion, and a variety of viewpoints. Such diversity strengthens the church and our witness in the world, as we have already explored and as, indeed, I have explored in depth, in the first *One for All* book. Unity on primary issues is essential. Most of us would agree on those principles. The problem arises when we try to work out what is primary and what is secondary. If we can make the former list as small as possible it will lead to a great quantitative unity and, some would argue, we should make the latter list as large as possible for the same reason. That is true – but it is not as simple as that.

Adiaphora

The term *adiaphora* is Greek in origin. It is a plural word which literally means "those things which are indifferent". In this context, "indifferent" does not mean not caring about something; instead it means that it is not morally or ethically important. The use of the term in this sense goes back to Stoic philosophy. According to the Stoics, all the objects human beings pursue during their lives can be divided into three classes. First, there are things that are good, such as virtue, wisdom, justice, temperance, and so forth. Second, there are things that are bad, such as vice, folly, injustice, and intemperance. Third, there are things such as wealth and fame that are in themselves neither good nor bad, but morally neutral, and in that sense *adiaphora*.

In subsequent Christian theology this concept of some things being in themselves morally neutral has been taken over to refer to those things which are neither specifically commanded nor specifically prohibited by God, and that is what is meant when Christian theologians talk about *adiaphora*. Therefore, for Christians, if something is *adiaphora*, it means that something is debatable, spiritually neutral. But how do we know which things are debatable or secondary and which are not? And, for my purposes, an important question is, can something be secondary while at the same time having a primary impact on unity?

In the New Testament, the discussion of how to behave in relation to things that are *adiaphora*[136] is to be found in three passages in the letters of Paul: Romans 14:1 – 15:13, 1 Corinthians 8, and 1 Corinthians 10:23–33, where the subject is discussed even though the word itself is not used. In order to understand these three passages correctly, we have to consider them against the background of the shift from the Old Covenant to the New that took place because of the life, death, and resurrection of Jesus Christ and the gift of the Holy Spirit. Paul's letter to the Ephesians helps us understand the fundamental shift that takes place through Christ that changes what is "essential" for the Christian:

> So then, remember that at one time you Gentiles by birth, called "the uncircumcision" by those who are called "the circumcision" – a physical circumcision made in the flesh by human hands – remember that you were at that time without Christ, being aliens from the commonwealth of Israel, and strangers to the covenants of promise, having no hope and without God in the world. But now in Christ Jesus you who once were far off have been brought near by the blood of Christ. For he is our peace; in his flesh he has made both groups into one and has broken down the dividing wall, that is, the hostility between us. He has abolished the law with its commandments and ordinances, so that he might create in himself one new humanity in place of the two, thus making peace, and might reconcile both groups to God in one body

through the cross, thus putting to death that hostility through it. So he came and proclaimed peace to you who were far off and peace to those who were near; for through him both of us have access in one Spirit to the Father. So then you are no longer strangers and aliens, but you are citizens with the saints and also members of the household of God, built upon the foundation of the apostles and prophets, with Christ Jesus himself as the cornerstone. In him the whole structure is joined together and grows into a holy temple in the Lord; in whom you also are built together spiritually into a dwelling-place for God.

Ephesians 2:11–22

That means that through Christ God has acted to abolish the division between Jews and Gentiles and to create one, new, holy people who have been reconciled to God through His Son. Christians have access to God the Father through the Spirit.

As part of this action, God has "abolished the law with its commandment and ordinances". In other words, He has abolished the requirement that God's people are defined by their adherence to the Mosaic Law, understood as a boundary marker separating Jew from Gentile. For Paul, God has fulfilled the requirement of the Old Covenant in the life and ministry of His Son, Jesus Christ. This means that some of the expectations of behaviour and conduct that have been placed upon the Jewish people have been fulfilled in Jesus Christ.

(a) The divine intention, as Paul saw it unveiled in the messianic events concerning Jesus, was to create a single worldwide family; and therefore any practices that functioned as symbols dividing

different ethnic groups could not be maintained as absolutes within this single family. Thus the major marks of Israel's ethnic distinctiveness – circumcision, food laws, Sabbath, and the Jerusalem Temple itself – were to be set aside, not because they were bad, not given by God, or representative of a shabby or second-rate kind of "religion," but because of "messianic eschatology," the fact that in Jesus Israel's God had at last done the new thing he had always promised. (b) This divine intention, glimpsed in Scriptures upon which Paul drew, and sketched out in much of his teaching, was that this single family would, by the Spirit's work, embody, represent and carry forward the plan of "new creation," the plan which had been the intention for Israel; and that therefore any practices that belonged to the dehumanizing, anticreation world of sin and death could likewise not be maintained within this new-creation family. The first principle explains why certain things are now "indifferent;" the second why certain things are not. This is the difference between the two kinds of "difference." We note that in this double edged ecclesiology Jewish believers are required to give up the absolutizing of their specific ethnic boundary markers, and erstwhile pagan believers are required to give up elements of their former life which they have taken for granted.[137]

The new community of Christ on Earth

Paul's appeal for unity across traditional boundaries is based on the absolutely essential understanding of the new community that has been created in the church through the work of Christ. Old social, cultural, religious, economic, and gender-based separations have been swallowed up by Christ. This means that those cultural separators that were once essential for the Jewish believing community, such as the eating of meat offered to idols and the observance of holy days, are now disputable matters. This is the very point that Paul makes in 1 Corinthians and in Romans. His point is not that behaviour no longer matters, or that holiness and faithfulness to God is optional. His point is that Jesus Christ, the Messiah, has fulfilled the ancient promises and therefore Christ's people, the church, can now be united in worship and rooted in mutual respect in such a way that they are able to handle differences in conviction and behaviour that flow from their cultural roots. "He does not ask the different groups to give up their practices; merely not to judge one another where differences exist."[138]

The truth is that sometimes it is easier to demand conformity of behaviour in secondary issues than it is to allow for a charitable understanding of one another. The decision to change one's view of an issue from obligatory to permissible is not easy. Seeing something as a secondary issue rather than a primary one is a hard transition. Issues such as the consumption of alcohol are a good example of what I am trying to articulate. In some communities, it would be seen as entirely contrary to Christian culture to drink alcohol, while in others it is seen as totally acceptable. The tensions between these two viewpoints can be very hard to navigate.

I travel widely and see regularly the impact of issues such as this. The challenge is to be committed to the unity of the church and so to be willing to accept the cultural context within which you find yourself at a given time and to be determined not to jump to a hasty judgment, so long as the behaviour you are seeing is not contrary to the teaching of the Scriptures. We must be careful not to insist that all other Christians conform at once to the freedoms which we might celebrate.[139] Calvin puts the issue thus:

In all cases we must study charity, and look to the edification
of our neighbour. "All things are lawful for me," says he, "but
all things are not expedient; all things are lawful for me,
but all things edify not. Let no man seek his own, but every
man another's wealth," (1 Cor. 10:23, 24). There is nothing
plainer than this rule, that we are to use our liberty if it tends
to the edification of our neighbour, but if inexpedient for our
neighbour, we are to abstain from it.[140]

Liberty is not licence

We are to use our liberty in such a way that it enables our sister or
brother to flourish. Styles of worship, preferences in gatherings,
observances of holy days, and so on are disputable. What matters
most is the acceptance of justification by faith and the love of one's
neighbour.[141] To borrow a phrase from the title of Martin Luther's
work of 1520, we are to celebrate the freedom of Christian faith
rather than impose rules and regulations on others that God has
not imposed upon them.[142]

The key to what is a disputable matter and what is not lies
in understanding that Paul is helping early believers to think in a
Christian way, that is to say, he gives them the tools to look at their
behaviour and their commitments through the lens of Christ's
fulfilling work:

He is teaching people to think messianically and especially
to think through their own faith and practice, and their
membership of the community with others on the same
journey but at different points along the road, in the light of
the Messiah's death and resurrection. He is teaching them to
navigate through difficult and only partly chartered waters,

with the Messiah and his saving death as the principal star by which they must steer. And in that situation the adiaphora is about as different from a modern doctrine of "tolerance" as can be imagined. "Tolerance" is not simply a low-grade version of "love"; in some senses, it is its opposite, as "tolerance" can imply a distancing, a wave from the other side of the street, rather than the embrace of "the sibling for whom the Messiah died".[143]

The idea of disputable matters helps us immensely as Christians to allow one another liberty in conscience, but we must not allow it to be a licence for whatever behaviour we like. The New Testament gives us the freedom to expect an attitude of loving liberty from one another, but it does not permit us to trample on one another's consciences. The principle of *adiaphora* strengthens unity in so far as it makes room for one another, within the context of the expectations of holy living set out in the Bible, but it does not disregard behaviour and conduct as irrelevant. So we accept that things change over time as the church grapples with new issues and faces new challenges and as new cultures become part of the Christian community.

Adiaphora does not become a new "anything goes" principle; instead, it allows us to assess situations from the context of mutual love and respect. That demands consistent effort and a willingness to listen to one another carefully and respect one another deeply, but it is important to note what is not included in disputable matters as well as what is. Paul never includes sexual ethics or other topics that can break relationship with one another or have an impact on how we perceive one another or honour one another as members of the new community of Christ as topics on which we can agree to disagree. His expectations of behaviour around marriage and sexual conduct are deeply and thoroughly grounded in the Jewish understanding of the former being a union of lifelong sexual faithfulness and monogamy between a man and a woman, and his teaching on the latter is grounded in the simple truth that any sexual intercourse outside of the parameters of marriage is wrong. The same can be said of expectations around lying, violence, lawsuits, and many other issues. For the early church, and for the church through the ages, those things that are disputable are those things that don't matter, not those things that are too difficult to discuss or too controversial to address.[144]

A new framework for unity

The impact on how we maintain unity today is profound. Those who are part of the family of God are part of Christ's body, filled by His Spirit, guided by His Word, and empowered for His purposes. We are a new covenant community and we are part of a new creation, demonstrating to the world what the kingdom of God looks like. This is the basis upon which we can discern how we live with differences of practice in areas for which the church has neither the right nor a mandate to approve or condone different positions. We are not a community that believes in truth in the abstract, however. We connect what we believe to how we live. The old lines of "liberal" and "conservative" are not particularly helpful for us as we navigate the contexts in which we find ourselves today. We cannot separate behaviour from belief.

We need a new framework for unity if we are to navigate the terrain in which we find ourselves. It is neither accurate nor fair for one side of the church to lay claim to adjectives such as progressive, open, welcoming, inclusive, affirming, and accepting and to imply that those who disagree with them on issues such as sexual ethics do not carry any of those characteristics. It is also not accurate or fair for one side of the church to lay claim to adjectives such as faithful, biblical, holy, obedient, and clear. There is no doubt that the current embodiment of this debate around what is primary and what is secondary, or what is permissible and what is required, is the issue of sexual ethics. We must do better in our language and conversation in this area. Our conversations are difficult, our divisions are clear, and our options are rather limited. Yet we must still hold to the reality of what it means to work this out together for as long as we can in the best way that we can.

Our theology of sexual practice does not, in and of itself, determine our salvation,[145] but how we handle the implications of our viewpoint on it is of the utmost significance. We cannot pretend it is not an issue, and we must not bury our heads in the sand over it. We must wrestle with it from a biblical and theological point of view that is rooted in the story of Christ and shaped by the will of God, not just by our preferences or desires. This may mean that division becomes inevitable, but that inevitability is determined by our willingness to engage in discussion with one another with Christ at the forefront of our minds, the teaching of Scripture shaping our thinking, and the presence and power of the Holy Spirit being our source.

As important as the issue of sexual ethics is today, however, there have been other issues in the past and there will be others in the future. We, the church, are confronted with decisions we must make in each generation. Our forebears grappled with issues of faithfulness, and the torchbearers of the future will too. Our responsibility is to protect the unity of the Spirit in the bond of peace. It isn't easy, but no one ever said that it would be. It is, however, essential. We must ask ourselves, what is fundamental to our unity and what is not? We build on Christ, as Christ's people, obedient to His ethics and shaped by His Word.

In the midst of our differences, there is a reality that we must not forget: before we are opponents in a battle of ideas or ethics, we are bound together as people in the body of Christ, and it is to this that we now turn.

Core Principles – Three Commitments for Unity

What principles can guide us as we think about protecting the unity that we have been given in Christ?[146] We have already explored a number of them, such as listening more effectively, adopting a code of conduct for unity, making sure we know the difference between disputable matters and matters that are essential, learning to disagree without being disagreeable, and understanding the differences between agreement and unity. We now turn to a series of helpful aides-memoires that can shape our relationships with one another. They are not complicated, but they do work and, if employed, can help us to defend and to strengthen our commitments to one another.

Earlier I suggested a code of conduct for unity. Now let me suggest some core values that might help us.

We put people before problems

It is so easy to define someone as a problem rather than as a person. This is particularly true when it comes to a person with whom we are in conflict. The issue we are addressing together becomes greater than the person in front of us. Such a viewpoint not only dehumanizes the person with whom we are engaged, but it also dehumanizes us.

I am always struck by the fact that Christ saw people. He knew their names; He listened to their stories. He was interested in the events of their lives. They mattered to Him. He did not label Mary as the prostitute but instead He knew her name. He became her friend. Matthew was not simply the tax collector. Zacchaeus was not the swindler. Christ saw people. He called people. He discipled people and He sends us to reach people. There is a beautiful picture of this in the story of the man who was possessed by a demon in the Gerasene region:[147]

> Then they arrived at the country of the Gerasenes, which is opposite Galilee. As he stepped out on land, a man of the city who had demons met him. For a long time he had worn no clothes, and he did not live in a house but in the tombs. When he saw Jesus, he fell down before him and shouted at the top of his voice, "What have you to do with me, Jesus, Son of the Most High God? I beg you, do not torment me" – for Jesus had commanded the unclean spirit to come out of the man. (For many times it had seized him; he was kept under guard and bound with chains and shackles, but he would break the bonds and be driven by the demon into the wilds.) Jesus then asked him, "What is your name?" He said, "Legion"; for many demons had entered him. They begged him not to order them to go back into the abyss.
>
> Now there on the hillside a large herd of swine was feeding; and the demons begged Jesus to let them enter these. So he gave them permission. Then the demons came out of the man and entered the swine, and the herd rushed down the steep bank into the lake and was drowned.

> *When the swineherds saw what had happened, they ran off and told it in the city and in the country. Then people came out to see what had happened, and when they came to Jesus, they found the man from whom the demons had gone sitting at the feet of Jesus, clothed and in his right mind. And they were afraid. Those who had seen it told them how the one who had been possessed by demons had been healed. Then all the people of the surrounding country of the Gerasenes asked Jesus to leave them; for they were seized with great fear. So he got into the boat and returned. The man from whom the demons had gone begged that he might be with him; but Jesus sent him away, saying, "Return to your home, and declare how much God has done for you." So he went away, proclaiming throughout the city how much Jesus had done for him.*
>
> Luke 8:26–39

The picture that is painted of this man prior to his encounter with Christ is of a person who has lost their identity and has been consigned to a living death, inhabiting a graveyard and hidden from the world.[148] He is a man without a name, without a story, and without a future – until he is met by the Lord Jesus. After that encounter he is calmed, welcomed, and included. He is found sitting at the feet of Jesus, clothed, and in his right mind.[149] Jesus takes people whose identity has been lost, or perhaps even those whose identity has never been known to them, and He gives them back their dignity. He personalizes the person.

In our striving to protect unity we must do the same. It is easy to label another person. Perhaps we do that so that our disagreements can be easier. After all, it is much easier to disagree and fall out of relationship with "the evangelicals" or "the liberals" than it is to do so with Malcolm, who is an evangelical, or with Janet, who is a liberal. We see this kind of depersonalization all the time in our discussions. We label people according to their colour, their gender, their disability, their denominational tribe, or their sexuality. Yet labels make it harder to love those who are different from us. If we are not careful, the label becomes a category, or a box, in which we lock people away. If we can label someone, we can define them, and if we can define them, we can work out how to control them, or keep them at arm's length. Learning to avoid labels is about learning to see the person before the problem. Unity is strengthened when we see people. By refusing to label someone we give them their dignity back – we personalize them – and by doing that we make schism more difficult. Human dignity is not something that people earn; it is a human right. All people carry that right, whoever they are and wherever they are from. We must be careful to afford people that right.

I have often found myself in conflict situations. It might be because I have said something in a sermon, a book, an article, or a lecture that someone has disagreed with. It is remarkable how seeing the person instead of the problem can help with avoiding unnecessary conflict. I was asked recently to unpack my pastoral position on divorce and remarriage.[150] At the end of the day, a very angry man came toward me with fire in his eyes. He was furious that I had outlined a position which, to him, seemed to be liberal and contrary to the teaching of Scripture. He was wagging his finger in my face and shouting at me. Instead of becoming defensive and countering his anger with my own, which I must confess is what I felt like doing, I stopped him. I then explained I would be happy to continue to engage with him but I first wanted to know his name and why he felt so strongly about this issue. He told me both, and in the course of doing so, I could see the person and not the problem. As it turned out, he felt strongly about the issue because his own parents had been divorced and his mother had taken an extremely hard line on the issue. This had shaped his own view. The decision to find out his name and to listen to his story was important: it changed the tone of the exchange. I was able to use his name in my replies. I was able to listen to him more carefully. It did not change his perspective on the issue, or mine, but it did change our perspective on one another. I find that using a person's name does that almost every time I face a conflict.

Jean Vanier is the founder of L'Arche, a community that brings together people with development disabilities and the friends and family who share their lives. He has discovered the reality that those whom others call weak can teach us a great deal about truth, spirituality, and God. He has discovered the power of knowing people. In knowing them, in naming them, in sharing life with them, we discover more of what unites us. In his letter of 1 September 1985 from Trolsy in France he wrote about the growing work of L'Arche and the communities he had recently visited:

In each place there was the joy of getting to know each person, of sharing a meal around the table, of praying together and of meeting the board of directors. So much life in each community; the laughter, the joy of being together, but also the deep pain in some people. I meet the same suffering everywhere I go for retreats and visits. I am more and more aware of the reality of anguish which is like an inner uneasiness, a feeling of death in the heart. It comes from a sense of being abandoned, of not being loved, of not having any place in society, in the family or in the community. Isn't it surprising that some of the last words of Jesus are "Why have you abandoned me?!" It is the primal cry of so many of our world today: "Why don't you love me?" "Why isn't there room for me?" And these questions lead to another one: "Whose fault is it?" "Am I bad or is it the fault of someone else?" We try to find the guilty one, or else we condemn ourselves.[151]

Something powerful happens when we choose to name another person. We enter their story. We become participants and not just observers. As a pastor, I have seen the power of this again and again. It is not unusual to meet someone who is apparently against the church, or against Christian faith, but when we dig deeper and listen to their story, we realize that they have actually been hurt by someone in the church and therefore they have been hurt by the church. By seeing the person and not the problem, we make a choice to enter the narrative and not simply to critique it.

Life is personal. By definition. All parts of it. Language, work, friends, family, flowers, vegetables, rocks and hills. Father, Son, and Holy Spirit – the works. When any part of life is abstracted from the particular, formulated into a generalisation, bureaucratized into a project, reduced to a cause, life itself is killed, or at least diminished considerably. When any one of us quits being personally present to our child, our spouse, or our friend, life leaks out.[152]

Learning to see a person and not a problem is a liberating principle. It puts an obstacle in the way of much of our pontification and reminds us that relationship sits at the heart of healthy community.

We put discussion above debate

We argue too much. I don't mean to suggest that disagreement is wrong or that confrontation is always bad. Far from it. Disagreement can sharpen our thinking immeasurably and help us to clarify our ideas and our commitments. Confrontation is not a bad thing.

I was recently engaged in a conversation with Nicky Morgan, a leading politician in the United Kingdom and a Christian. The context was that Nicky was part of a panel discussion at Spring Harvest in which we were exploring what it meant to disagree well. She is a member of the Conservative party and has had her own disagreements within the party. She campaigned to remain in the United Kingdom in the referendum that was held in June 2016 on whether or not the country should leave the European Union. In my discussion with her, she pointed out the need for healthy opposition in a democracy. When difference, discussion, and dialogue are absent or stifled, we end up with weaker decisions and poorer thinking, she commented. We then went on to explore the kind of thinking and discussion that is most helpful. Nicky reflected that when we become too adversarial, we lose something. In her view, that is why instruments such as referenda themselves are blunt and unhelpful instruments. They polarize people and societies precisely because they become arguments rather than discussions.

Too many conflicts in our churches and in our homes are managed as arguments and debates rather than as discussions. Debates and arguments have winners and losers, whereas discussions have participants. Debates are often predicated upon someone being right and someone being wrong, whereas discussions are predicated upon people having different opinions. In debates, arguments are made and responded to, but in discussions, points are made and developed and shaped by dialogue. When we debate, we are adversarial – in fact, we often face one another, as they do the in the House of Commons and the House of Lords – but in discussions, we sit in a round, we lean into one another. There are many other differences.[153] One of the things that I think is most helpful about dialogues as opposed to debates is that they invite others into them and they enable us to think through issues for ourselves.

There is no doubt that there are many areas where the church is called to have a specific position on an issue, as outlined in the previous chapter, but it is also true to say that there are many areas on which the church does not have one position, but rather that there are a number of ways of understanding the subject within the Christian family. Take as an example the issue of creation. There is more than one way of reading faithfully the book of Genesis. Some Christians believe it to be a literal account of creation, others see it as figurative, and still others see it as liturgical in character. Which is right? What are the implications of each view? How do they work out across the rest of the Scriptures? I have found it extremely helpful, when teaching on a subject such as this, to provide a context and a space for a dialogue between two opposing views. Congregations and audiences find it extremely helpful to see disagreement modelled in dialogue rather than in pedagogy. I wonder how many other issues in theology and in Christian spirituality would benefit from a dialogical approach to differences. I can think of a number that would benefit from this approach, such as how and why we pray, the place and characteristics of worship, eschatology, mission, and how and why we read the Bible, to name but a few.

For the 2017 Spring Harvest event, the Planning Group decided that we would introduce a main session as part of the day that allowed a dialogue across different specialists and invited guests rather than just a presentation by one person. The session was entitled "One for All", and included interviews, conversations, questions from the floor, and ten-minute presentations from speakers. Contributors included the Archbishop of Canterbury, leading politicians, the General Director of the Evangelical Alliance, and one of the directors from the global charity World Vision. It was a huge success. Guests found it extremely helpful to be able to listen to a conversation and to draw their own conclusions as they listened prayerfully with open Bibles on their laps. They were helped to think through for themselves the subjects being discussed. I have a feeling that the learning they experienced as a result will be much more embedded in their minds and their wills.

Putting discussion above debate does not mean that we will not disagree. Far from it. Discussing something rather than debating it can take much more time and energy and can be much more frustrating. As a family of six, we often joke that when we have a discussion about where to eat it takes six times as long as it would if we were to just let one person decide! The point is not to avoid conflict; rather it is to ensure that we have healthy, participative relationships in which we listen to one another well.

As the leader of a large Baptist church, I am used to discussions. We work in an ecclesiological model that believes that the major decisions of the church family should be made together. This slows some things down, but it also makes sure that we are travelling with one another. Sometimes it can end up being too circular, and someone, often one of our elders or pastors, needs to remind the community that we cannot talk about an issue for ever. On the whole, though, the process of dialogue and listening to one another means that our decisions are made more effectively, carry more weight, and have greater longevity and impact because we have thought things through together and made the decision together. We do not vote on many things, as we think that the rush to democracy in many Baptist churches actually misses the point of our ecclesiology. Instead, we come together in the church meeting to seek the mind of God as one. We listen for His voice as we listen to one another. That means our times together in church meetings involve prayer, allowing room for the Holy Spirit to speak to us in worship, study, and the use of the gifts of the Holy Spirit, and creating the space to hear one another through open discussion and reflection. It also means that our church meetings can be long! Yet it works for us because all who are part of the church family have a part to play.

We are led by an eldership. That means that, as a church family, we have recognized the need to have a group of people who lead us. At the moment we have fifteen women and men in our eldership. We work together and share responsibility for the direction and vision of the church and we are accountable to the church meeting. We discuss discipline, spirituality, biblical curriculum, mission, evangelism, strategic direction, and the theological convictions we hold as individuals, as leaders, and as a church family. I lead that team but operate as a first among equals. It works. In both our church meetings and our meetings as elders, we have learned the art of listening to one another, not just of being quiet while someone else is speaking.

We put being united above being right

To genuinely listen means that we acknowledge that the other person's point of view is valid and that it may have something that can help me understand an issue more clearly or vice versa. As the lead pastor at Gold Hill, I have to work hard at giving permission for this kind of community. I am frustrated that many people still look to me to tell them what to think. This happens in our staff team, in our eldership, and across the church family. I have to make a choice to resist the temptation to bypass the discussion elements of our decision processes to save myself time. Even if the decision that we end up making is one that I could have predicted, it doesn't mean that we can jump to it without the process of listening to one another well. A community is stronger, and is certainly more united, when we place discussion and listening as high priorities.

What is the point of winning an argument but losing a relationship unless the point at the heart of the argument is of the utmost importance?[154] I am challenged by the determination of Christ to maintain His relationship with His disciples even when He knew that Judas would betray Him. Christ remained committed to Judas, even when Judas had rejected Christ. On the night that He was betrayed, Jesus not only washed Judas's feet, but He also served him bread and wine and included him in a sacred act of love:

> *Now before the festival of the Passover, Jesus knew that his hour had come to depart from this world and go to the Father. Having loved his own who were in the world, he loved them to the end. The devil had already put it into the heart of Judas son of Simon Iscariot to betray him. And during supper Jesus,*

knowing that the Father had given all things into his hands, and that he had come from God and was going to God, got up from the table, took off his outer robe, and tied a towel around himself. Then he poured water into a basin and began to wash the disciples' feet and to wipe them with the towel that was tied around him...

After saying this Jesus was troubled in spirit, and declared, "Very truly, I tell you, one of you will betray me." The disciples looked at one another, uncertain of whom he was speaking. One of his disciples – the one whom Jesus loved – was reclining next to him; Simon Peter therefore motioned to him to ask Jesus of whom he was speaking. So while reclining next to Jesus, he asked him, "Lord, who is it?" Jesus answered, "It is the one to whom I give this piece of bread when I have dipped it in the dish." So when he had dipped the piece of bread, he gave it to Judas son of Simon Iscariot. After he received the piece of bread, Satan entered into him. Jesus said to him, "Do quickly what you are going to do." Now no one at the table knew why he said this to him. Some thought that, because Judas had the common purse, Jesus was telling him, "Buy what we need for the festival"; or, that he should give something to the poor. So, after receiving the piece of bread, he immediately went out. And it was night.

John 13:1–6, 21–30

We assume that to be right means that we will be in the ascendency or that our argument will win the day, but that is not always the case. Jesus did not put being right above loving His disciples. He loved them unconditionally, just as He loves us unconditionally. That doesn't mean in any way that what we think, believe, or do doesn't matter to Him. Just as He challenged Judas,[155] James and John,[156] and Peter,[157] He challenges our behaviour and our attitudes, but He does so without breaking relationship with us. It was while we were still in sin that Christ died for us,[158] and we must always remember that He loved us first[159] and that He is more committed to us than we are to Him. He promises never to leave us.[160] He will not break relationship with us, and remains committed to interceding for us now, despite our refusal to follow His ways and obey His commands.[161]

It is much easier to walk away from someone when they hurt us than it is to remain committed to them. Over my years as a Christian, I have hurt other people and I have been hurt by them. Sometimes that has caused a break in relationship. I wish I could say that I have always made the right call on this principle, that I have stuck with a commitment to love someone even when we deeply disagree, but I know that in the early years of my Christian faith that was not always the case. I allowed disagreements about doctrine to create a no-man's-land between me and a brother or sister. My need to be right and to be vindicated was greater than my need to keep loving them. I am learning to let the emphasis be the other way round, though.

Almost thirty years ago, a fellow Christian, who was also one of my leaders, disagreed with my decision to study theology at university. He cut us off from himself and from the church we were then part of. The division lasted twenty years. My wife and I made a choice: we would not allow the actions of those who had hurt us to stop us loving them. So we wrote to them regularly and prayed for them often. We consistently brought the issue back to the cross and made a decision to forgive them. Almost twenty years after the initial hurt was caused, God turned it around. In a humanly unplanned way, the individual concerned and I met at a conference where I was speaking, and we were able to talk about the conflict and resolve the issue. It was hard to keep loving him through those years. It took a steady and consistent decision to see him as Christ saw him and to put seeing our relationship being restored above being right, but it was worth it.

As we come to the end of this, our penultimate, chapter, ask yourself if there are situations where you are putting the need to be right above the need to be in relationship. As long as you are in relationship with someone, you can communicate. You don't have to sacrifice your principles, you don't have to dilute your commitment to the truth, you just have to love harder. I have proven the principle of love in my own life many times. In my personal life, in my life as a pastor and as a church leader, and in my life in the public sphere I have discovered that consistent love breaks down the barriers that people build to keep me out. Loving someone unconditionally is a powerful force for good and a powerful witness to the world:

> *Let love be genuine; hate what is evil, hold fast to what is good; love one another with mutual affection; outdo one another in showing honour. Do not lag in zeal, be ardent in spirit, serve the Lord. Rejoice in hope, be patient in suffering, persevere in prayer. Contribute to the needs of the saints; extend hospitality to strangers.*
>
> *Bless those who persecute you; bless and do not curse them. Rejoice with those who rejoice, weep with those who weep. Live in harmony with one another; do not be haughty, but associate with the lowly; do not claim to be wiser than you are. Do not repay anyone evil for evil, but take thought for what is noble in*

the sight of all. If it is possible, so far as it depends on you, live peaceably with all. Beloved, never avenge yourselves, but leave room for the wrath of God; for it is written, "Vengeance is mine, I will repay, says the Lord." No, "if your enemies are hungry, feed them; if they are thirsty, give them something to drink; for by doing this you will heap burning coals on their heads." Do not be overcome by evil, but overcome evil with good.

Romans 12:9–21

Perhaps we think we have to fight our own battles? Perhaps we have allowed ourselves to be convinced that the honour of God's name and purpose is wholly dependent upon us? Perhaps we are worried that people around us will get away with wrong behaviours and attitudes and therefore we have to see justice done and their sinfulness exposed? Maybe we are just hurt that someone is allowed to hurt us? There are lots of reasons that explain why we want to win arguments, but there is one strong and clear reason why, in the end, we should put loving other people and keeping the door open to them above having to be right. God did it for us. He accepted, loved, and welcomed us before we changed our way of thinking. He loves us even when we argue with Him. We may choose to walk away from Him, but He will never walk away from us.

Sometimes the hardest thing to do is to let someone walk away. We pursue them, we love them, and we leave the door open for them, but they reject us. John Wesley never left the Anglican Church, but they walked away from him. Jesus did not reject the Jewish people; they rejected Him. We cannot control whether others accept our love or are open to our desire to stay in relationship with them, but we can refuse to reject them.

These three principles are powerful tools in the armoury of unity: we put people before problems, we put discussion above debate, and we put being united above being right. As we navigate the challenges of unity, these core commitments, these central values, will help us to hold on to the unity that God has given to us. If we have to divide, and perhaps this is an inevitability because of our fallen natures, then let the way in which we divide become a gift to the world around us in and of itself. Unity doesn't always prevail. There are some choices that people make that mean we have to challenge them publicly, but we should always do so lovingly. We must never revel in our divisions. We must never point to them as proof of our faithfulness over and against the unfaithfulness of someone else. We must not crow and strut in our rightness. Division, when it happens, is heartbreaking to God and should be heartbreaking to us. We must not trumpet our purity with a glint in our eye that betrays a heart of pride. Where division is the result of a stand for truth, a commitment to the gospel, and a readiness to defend the cross, we know we are doing the right thing, but let us never, ever think that God rejoices in the division. He may rejoice in our willingness to suffer for Him, but His heart breaks that we have to.

In a world that is becoming increasingly fractured and where division is becoming an easy and pain-free option, we can make our divisions themselves a gift. We can show the world that schism is always sore, that division carries in it the seeds of destruction if we are not careful, and that fracture is wrought with pain. We were not made to be alone, and we were not made to be divided.

May God help us to remember the reason why we should always protect our unity. And so we come to our final chapter.

One for Purpose

Our unity is not for its own sake. It has a glorious purpose, which is that "the world may know" that the Father has sent the Son as the Saviour.[162]

"I ask not only on behalf of these, but also on behalf of those who will believe in me through their word, that they may all be one. As you, Father, are in me and I am in you, may they also be in us, so that the world may believe that you have sent me. The glory that you have given me I have given them, so that they may be one, as we are one, I in them and you in me, that they may become completely one, so that the world may know that you have sent me and have loved them even as you have loved me."

John 17:20–23

I have no doubt that there is a place and, to some extent, a power in the variety of expressions of Christian distinctiveness that we see in denominations across the world. Each one adds another dimension to the rich tapestry of the body of Christ. And yet we cannot avoid the clear and clarion call of Jesus in John 17 that the unity He prays for will be manifested to the world. It will be visible. It will be tangible.[163] As I have said repeatedly, we do not strive for unity for the sake of unity; rather we live out of unity because it is a gift that God has given to us, and we remember that unity itself has a missional impact. Our unity is a witness to the world that a community can live together with difference and with hope. The church of Jesus Christ is a powerful witness to the world that we can find one another across cultural, social, political, ethnic, gender, economic, and educational divides.

One across the world

We are one across the world. When one part of the church is persecuted, we are all persecuted. When one part of the church is in revival, the whole church is blessed. In any given twenty-four-hour period, around 100,000 people begin a new life in Jesus Christ. That is something that we can celebrate. In Europe we are facing huge challenges in the church, but we must somehow remember that we are part of a global family. We are united across the world and we are united for the world.

I have often discovered the great blessing of visiting another culture, another country, and another community and feeling at home. I have sat with the persecuted sister or brother in Iraq, in Vietnam, in Indonesia, and seen the joy of the light of Christ in them. A powerful thing happens in us when we realize that we are part of a worldwide family. Our perspectives change and our priorities are reordered. The ease and wealth and abundance that we have is recalibrated when we discover the lack and the need in our brothers and sisters. This global unity causes us to see that we could make a difference in the lives of our Christian family around the world if we would only open our hearts a little more and release our resources a little more readily.

There is more to our global unity than just sharing our resources with others. We also receive so much from others. We see the fallacy of theologies that avoid suffering. We are reminded of the reality of spiritual battle and the power of evil in the world. When we remember the global church we are less willing to allow our theological preferences to become so strong that they actually threaten the physical well-being of our brothers and sisters in other lands. Our global unity means that when one part of the body of Christ is struggling, another part that is prospering can lift our spirits and lift our eyes. Our global unity means that we can learn new ways of doing mission, new models of church, new ideas of discipleship, and new avenues for service. As I write, my church family is preparing to learn from mission partners we have in China how to develop a better model of discipleship, and we are developing new partnerships with a church-planting movement from the United States. We have relationships with more than 300 churches across the United Kingdom and around sixty in the United States through a mission movement we enable. We learn from one another. We celebrate one another and we grow as we listen to one another and sit at one another's feet.

I also wonder whether the growing global crisis of displaced people around the world is an opportunity for the global church to shine. We have the resources and the creativity to be a major source of good in the world as people flee one country to find hope and safety in another. My prayer is that the opportunity will be matched by intentionality and will. The church of the Lord Jesus Christ in the world across the next fifty to seventy years may well find that our economic centre lies in the northern hemisphere while our spiritual centre lies in the southern hemisphere. What will we do about that? How can I, as a local church pastor, demonstrate my commitment to the global church? Surely I can do so through intentional global partnerships around mission and evangelism? Surely I can do so through investing in the parts of God's family that need our finances, our vision, and our experience? Surely I can learn from the models of mission, discipleship, and evangelism around the world? The global prayer movement can inspire me, and the global need can force me to my knees. And surely I can stand with my persecuted brothers and sisters around the world in solidarity?

As I do these things, and as I commit to the global church, I soon discover that our unity is strengthened and my focus on what really matters is sharpened.

We are one for the world.

One across the denominations

We are also one across the tribes of the Christian family. Notwithstanding the deep challenges of theological unity that exist between streams and traditions in the church, we are all called to proclaim Christ. As we lift Him up, the world is changed. It is as we focus on the unity we find in Him, the identity that flows from Him, and the mercy and hope that we receive through Him that we discover new energy and purpose.

I am utterly convinced that the age of the denomination is dying. I don't mean that I think it doesn't matter, but I do think that it matters less than we have thought. There is a generation rising in the church that has little to no concern for whether they are Anglican or Baptist or Pentecostal. The old factions and the old dividing lines are being dissolved by the water of the Spirit and the power of the blood of the Lord Jesus. Denominational structures are way behind what the Spirit is doing. We need fresh, new, and exciting ways of celebrating one another's ordained local leaders, of releasing one another to minister into the different tribes. We need better methods of theological education that see us pooling our resources, sharing our ideas, and dreaming together – but we can do it. We need to see a fresh wave of dreamers and visionaries who think beyond the denominational boundaries of what was and look into the horizon of what could be. Our identity as Christians is far more important than our denominational tags; it always has been.

Local churches are learning what it means to unite around the common cause and purpose in Christ rather than the old-style denominational affiliations. At the church I lead, we share resources, training, mission, and ministry with churches in the area from other traditions. Most people in Gold Hill don't describe themselves as Baptists; they describe themselves as Christians, and they delight in the unity of heart and purpose they find with other Christians in our community. We work together, we weep together, and we dream together because we are one family.

If the church can embrace this deep-seated unity, we can be a greater witness in the world. I do not mean we need to abandon our differences or that we need to be a single united church denomination. Such organizational efforts are always a human construct and lead to greater division and dissatisfaction for most people at most levels. I mean we need to grasp the opportunities for mission that unity brings, such as a united voice into our communities, a shared sense of ownership in meeting the needs of our communities, so we can have specializations in each local church and a shared sense of mission and evangelism together. All of the churches in a local community can have a powerful impact in events, in evangelism, in outreach into schools and nursing homes and hospitals and businesses when we work together.

We are one for a purpose.

One across the generations

We are one across all ages. The children and young people of our communities need to see that we can make room for them. They need to know that there is a community that welcomes them, and so do those who are older. One of the greatest blights of our age is the isolation felt by older people, and another is the alienation felt by younger people. Again and again I have seen these two groups discover one another in the church. When you see older people mentoring younger people and younger people inspiring and enlivening older people, your heart sings. Recently in one of our services a mum with a young family gave me a note to read to our church. It said:

> Our children don't have Christian grandparents; they need you. We don't have Christian parents; we need you.

It was a powerful moment as our church realized that age is nothing but a number in our heads. We can be a community of sons and daughters, of mums and dads, of aunts and uncles. It is our failure to break down age and generational barriers in our churches that has caused so many people to step away from the church.

In the United Kingdom, we face a crisis in reaching young people and children. Almost half of those who are under the age of twenty-one and are Christians live in London. There are 72 per cent of churches that have no young people in them.[164] Only 32 per cent of young people said they believe in God in recent research. A total of 61 per cent of young people said that they knew a Christian, but only 18 per cent said they would be interested in finding out more about the Christian faith.[165] In the "Loosing Heart" research project carried out by Youthscape, only 50.2 per cent of those churches that were surveyed said they often discussed the basics of the Christian faith with their young people.[166] James Emery White said:

> *Times have changed. Culture has shifted dramatically. Unless [we] reach the next generation, the church will simply get older and smaller, year by year, until it is a shell of what it once was.*[167]

If we lose the battle for the church of Jesus Christ to be one across the generations, then we have lost the battle for the future of a vibrant, life-giving church in our culture. We know Jesus has promised that He will build His church and that the gates of Hades will not prevail against it,[168] but that does not mean that the future of the church as an effective witness in the UK or anywhere else is secure. For that to be the case, we must take responsibility for what is happening in our generation and for laying foundations for the generations to come. The church is never more than one generation away from collapse.[169]

Yet the church is a community for all ages, where one generation declares the praises of God to another.[170] We have a mandate from God to reach all ages with the powerful and life-giving message of the gospel, but we need one another to do it.

We are one for a purpose.

Hope for the future

I am optimistic about the future of the church. That optimism flows from my own personal experience. Across the world I see and experience a beautiful and vibrant community of people whose spirits are undaunted and whose vision is undimmed. Ordinary Christians are determined to put God first, to find one another, and to discover new and innovative ways of making Christ known. That optimism also flows from the reality that the church of Jesus Christ continues to grow every day. In addition, it flows from the theological conviction that God wins. One day, the knowledge of the glory of the Lord will cover the earth as the waters cover the sea.[171] That reality, the deep promise of God that He will put all things right, draws me forward. God has a people from every tongue and tribe and nation,[172] and He will have His way. Lastly, I am optimistic because I feel a deep frustration in my bones. It is the frustration that comes from vision, a vision of a church that is living out of its unity more than its division, a church that puts Christ before our petty divisions and disagreements, a church that yearns for the world to see and know Jesus. I do not want to lose the frustration because if I do, I will also lose the vision. There are millions of people like me: you are almost certainly one of them, otherwise you wouldn't have read this book!

Thank you for all you do for the kingdom of God. May we press in, together, to God's purposes and plans. May we commit ourselves to the vision of a church that is united in mission, heart, and purpose so that the world might know who Jesus is, why He came, and the difference He makes in our lives.

Notes

Crossing Barriers

1.   Tom Kraeuter, 1994. If Standing Together Is So Great, Why Do We Keep Falling Apart?: *Real Answers to Walking in Unity* (Hillsboro, MO: Emerald Books, 2001).

2.   See D. Bonhoeffer and J. W. Doberstein, *Life together* (Vol. 27; London: SCM Press, 1954). Bonhoeffer presents a powerful and moving argument for community that flows from love of one another. His arguments are all the more powerful given that in 1931 he returned to Germany from the United States of America and that he was eventually executed in Germany just before the end of the Second World War. He was a strong advocate of love and community but was also deeply troubled by the Nazi regime and became involved in a plot to kill Hitler. For Bonhoeffer, his love of the community and of truth and justice meant that he had to take a stand against the Nazis. Unity is not simply always accepting the behaviour and attitudes of others as valid; it sometimes involves challenging those behaviours and attitudes for the common good.

3.   See Luke 10:27; Matthew 22:37–39; Mark 12:30–31. Jesus is quoting from the Hebrew Scriptures – see also Deuteronomy 6:5 and Leviticus 19:18.

4.   See John 13:34–35.

5.   See Matthew 5:43–48.

6.   The full address of Bill Clinton at Martin McGuinness's funeral can be seen at "Bill Clinton's speech at Martin McGuinness' funeral in full – video", available at https://www.theguardian.com/uk-news/video/2017/mar/23/bill-clinton-speech-martin-mcguinness-funeral-full-video (last visited 6 June 2017). The funeral was a remarkable example of people from different sides of the religious and political landscapes in Northern Ireland coming together. It is a powerful call to unity, peace-building, and being willing to be part of the solution and not just identify the problem.

7. "Bill Clinton's speech at Martin McGuinness' funeral in full – video". This comment comes toward the end of Clinton's eulogy.

8. 1 Corinthians 15:3–4. This is, perhaps, the clearest and most succinct definition of the Gospel in the writings of the Apostle Paul.

9. See Malcolm Duncan, *One for All: The Foundations* (Oxford: Monarch Books, 2017).

10. Duncan, *One for All*, pp. 55ff.

11. Duncan, *One for All*, pp. 17f.

12. For a fuller unpacking of these central aspects of evangelicalism see D. W. Bebbington, *Evangelicalism in Modern Britain: A History from the 1730s to the 1980s* (Routledge, 2003).

13. See www.eden.co.uk/shop/search.php?q=Spring+HArvest+2017 to explore the resources available (last visited 6 June 2017).

14. Sim is the lead pastor of Freedom Church in Romsey and is a member of the Spring Harvest leadership team. You can find out more about him and his church family at http://www.freedomchurch.uk/ (last visited 6 June 2017).

15. You can access this declaration at "Spring Harvest 2017 Media", available at http://www.springharvest.org/2017media/ (last visited 8 June 2017).

16. See Luke 23:32–43, particularly verses 32 and 39–43.

17. "My sons have enjoyed building with Lego blocks since they were barely old enough to say 'Legos'. They especially like the sets that have all of the pieces for building a certain thing – a castle, a car, a boat, whatever. On the cover of such sets is a photo of what the project will look like when it is assembled correctly. Inside the box are step-by-step instructions on how to build it. The company has really tried to make it very easy. There is one minor problem, however. On the back of the box are usually four or five other photos of things you can build with the same pieces. Unfortunately, there are no instructions for these. You have to figure it out on your own. Sometimes that can be a major challenge." See Kraeuter, *If Standing Together is so Great, Why Do We Keep Falling Apart?* p. 14.

God's Plea

18.   This chapter appeared in *One for All: The Foundations* under the same title, pp. 55ff.

19.   Based on 1 Corinthians 1:10.

20.   Based on Ephesians 4:11–13.

21.   Based on Romans 12:4.

22.   Based on Colossians 3:13–14.

23.   Based on John 17:20–23.

24.   Based on Psalm 133.

25.   Based on 1 Peter 3:8.

26.   Based on Ephesians 4:3.

27.   Based on 1 John 4:12.

28.   Based on Romans 12:16.

29.   Based on Matthew 23:8.

30.   Based on Ephesians 2:14.

31.   Based on Philippians 2:1–11.

32.   Based on Galatians 3:26–28.

33.   Based on 1 Corinthians 12:12–13.

34.   Based on Ephesians 4:16.

35.   Based on Romans 6:5.

36.   Based on 1 Corinthians 1:10.

"In Him"

37.   For a further unpacking of some of the theological convictions of the importance of being in Christ, please see the chapter entitled "The Bedrock of Paul's Conviction – We Are One" in Duncan, *The Foundations*, pp.132–146.

38.   See J. Elsner, "Pausanias: A Greek Pilgrim in the Roman World", *Past and Present*, 135 (1992), pp. 3–29.

39. Stoicism was a school of Hellenistic philosophy that flourished throughout the Roman and Greek world until the third century AD. It is predominantly a philosophy of personal ethics which is informed by its system of logic and its views on the natural world. According to its teachings, the path to happiness for humans, as social beings, is found by accepting that which we have been given in life, by not allowing ourselves to be controlled by our desire for pleasure or our fear of pain, by using our minds to understand the world around us, by doing our part in nature's plan, and by working together and treating others in a fair and just manner.

40. Cynicism was a Greek philosophy of the fourth century BC which advocated the doctrines that virtue is the only good, that the essence of virtue is self-control and individual freedom, and that surrender to any external influence is beneath the dignity of man.

41. The Isthmian Games were a festival of athletic and musical competitions in honour of the sea god Poseidon, held in the spring of the second and fourth years of each Olympiad at his sanctuary on the Isthmus of Corinth. Legend attributed their origin either to Sisyphus, king of Corinth, or to Theseus. The Games were open to all Greeks and were especially popular with Athenians. The winner's prize was originally a crown of dry wild celery but was changed to a pine wreath in Roman times because pine was considered sacred to Poseidon. Celebration of the festival died out when Christianity became dominant in the fourth century AD.

42. For an excellent outline of the culture and context of Corinth, see Gordon D. Fee, *The First Epistle to the Corinthians* (Grand Rapids: Wm. B. Eerdmans, 1993), pp. 1–16.

43. See 2 Timothy 1:9.

44. See Ephesians 1:4.

45. See Romans 8:38–39.

46. See Ephesians 1:7.

47. See 2 Corinthians 5:21.

48. See 2 Corinthians 5:17.

49. See Ephesians 2:6.

50.   See 2 Corinthians 1:20.

51.   See 1 Corinthians 1:2.

52.   See Philippians 4:9.

53.   See Philippians 4:7.

54.   See Romans 6:23.

55.   See 1 Corinthians 15:22.

56.   John Piper, "The Stupendous Reality of being 'in Christ Jesus'", available at http://www.desiringgod.org/articles/the-stupendous-reality-of-being-in-christ-jesus (last visited 6 June 2017).

57.   See Acts 17:28 which contains Paul's famous address to the Athenians at Mars Hill.

Protecting Unity

58.   Church of England, *Grace and Disagreement: Shared Conversations on Scripture, Mission and Human Sexuality*, Vol. 1: "Thinking Through the Process" (London, 2014).

59.   Martin Luther, "Against the Roman Papacy, an Institution of the Devil" (1545) in *Luther's Works* (Vol. 41), edited by Eric W. Gritsch (Philadelphia: Fortress, 1966) p. 288. Luther was renowned for his polemic use of metaphor and insults. To see some of them, visit the website www.ergofabulous.org/luther (last visited 7 June 2017) where you can read them, with full citations, and even have the chance to hit a button with the words, "Insult me again", and be shown more and more of the reformer's insults.

60.   It is interesting to see the significant change of tone toward Luther under recent papacies, not least that of the current Pope, Francis. He has said that Luther's aim "was to renew the Church, not divide Her", and has described the Reformation as a "significant step", that "gave us courage", for the journey of inter-church dialogue. See "Pope Francis: Martin Luther wanted to 'renew the Church, not divide her'", *Catholic Herald*, 19 January 2017, available at http://www.catholicherald.co.uk/news/2017/01/19/pope-francis-martin-luther-wanted-to-renew-the-church-not-divide-her/ (last visited 7 June 2017).

61. Andrew Atherstone and Andrew Goddard, "Disagreeing with Grace", pp. 1–21 in *Good Disagreement? Grace and Truth in a Divided Church*, edited by Andrew Atherstone and Andrew Goddard (Oxford: Lion Books, 2015), p. 2. The quotation of Justin Welby is from Andrew Atherstone, *Archbishop Justin Welby: Risk-taker and Reconciler* (London: Darton, Longman and Todd, 2014), p. 210.

62. Atherstone and Goddard, "Disagreeing with Grace", p. 2.

63. I explore the example of the Patristics, particularly in North Africa, when it comes to the importance of guarding the unity of the church and learning how to disagree well in *The Foundations*, pp. 44–54.

64. I don't propose to address these questions and others like them in detail here. Some of them are covered in *The Foundations*. I give a sizeable part of that book to the issue of sexuality (see pp. 98–114) as I unpack the prayer of Jesus in John 17. My aim here is to try to set out some principles and practical steps that we can take to protect unity rather than address each individual issue. That would take another book!

65. See Ephesians 4:3.

66. One friend, who called to encourage me when the decision was made, quipped that I should rejoice in the fact that the vote was not 100 per cent because, according to Luke 6:26, "Woe to you when all speak well of you, for that is what their ancestors did to false prophets"!

67. The Baptist Union of Great Britain in reality is fundamentally responsible for the Baptist Union churches in England. It has always struck me as an inaccurate description of its remit. The Baptist Union of England would be a much more accurate description.

68. I recently delivered a keynote address on this issue to the Elim Leaders' Summit entitled "Same Spirit, Different Paradigm". Copies are available on request from me, via malcolm.duncan@goldhill.org.

69. For the text see http://www.vatican.va/roman_curia/pontifical_councils/chrstuni/documents/rc_pc_chrstuni_doc_31101999_cath-luth-joint-declaration_en.html (last visited 7 June 2017).

70. For helpful discussions of the implications of the issue of justification by faith through grace in the light of the Joint Declaration, see the following:

M. Root, "Aquinas, Merit, and Reformation Theology after the Joint Declaration on the Doctrine of Justification", *Modern Theology, 20 (1)* (2004), pp. 5–22.

W. G. Rusch and G. A. Lindbeck, *Justification and the Future of the Ecumenical Movement: The Joint Declaration on the Doctrine of Justification* (Liturgical Press, 2003).

L. Turcescu, "Soteriological Issues in the 1999 Lutheran–Catholic Joint Declaration on Justification: An Orthodox Perspective", *Journal of Ecumenical Studies, 38 (1)* (2001), p. 64.

C. J. Malloy, 2005. "Engrafted into Christ: A Critique of the Joint Declaration" (Vol. 233; Peter Lang, 2001).

T. M. Dorman, 2001. "The Joint Declaration of the Doctrine of Justification: Retrospect and Prospects", *Journal of the Evangelical Theological Society, 44(3)*, p. 421.

71.   Some of the theological building blocks for my suggestions here are laid out in *The Foundations*, pp. 151–162.

72.   Complementarianism is a theological view held by some in Christianity, Judaism, and Islam, that men and women have different but complementary roles and responsibilities in marriage, family life, religious leadership, and elsewhere. The word "complementary" and its cognates are currently used to denote this view.

73.   David Pawson, *Leadership is Male* (Highland, 1988).

74.   Anne Graham, *Womanhood Revisited: A Fresh Look at the Role of Women in Society* (Christian Focus, 2002).

75.   I use the term "egalitarian" to denote the conviction that there are no biblical gender-based restrictions on ministry in the church.

76.   See Philippians 3:2, 18 where the Apostle describes his opponents as dogs, as evildoers, and as mutilators of the flesh. He tells the Philippians that those whom he is describing have a destiny of destruction, have made their stomachs their gods, and have exchanged their glory for their shame. He tells the Philippians that such people have set their eyes on earthly things.

77.   For example, see Acts 8:20 where Peter tells those who think they can buy the blessing of God that they and their money deserve to be in hell. In 2 Peter 2:12, Peter describes those who are opposing the gospel (and remember they were claiming to be people of the gospel) as no better than ignorant animals who were born to be destroyed. Jude reminds his readers (verse 4) that those who were perverting the truth in their community were destined for destruction. 2 John 1:7 makes it clear that anyone who seeks to set up their view or themselves as alternatives to Christ are antichrists, where the prefix "anti" denotes a false replacement or alternative. When Jesus speaks to one of the churches through John, as recorded in Revelation 2:9, Jesus describes them as the "synagogue of Satan".

78.   See Matthew 3:7 and Luke 3:7.

79.   See Matthew 12:34, 23:33, and Matthew 23:16–17, 27.

80.   See John 8:44.

81.   See Mark 8:33.

82.   Atherstone and Goddard, "Disagreeing with Grace", p. 5.

83.   John Stott, *Christ the Controversialist: A Study in Some Essentials of Evangelical Religion* (Inter-Varsity Press, 1970), pp. 19–20.

84.   See Malcolm Duncan, *Unbelievable: Confident Faith in a Sceptical World* (Oxford: Monarch Books, 2014), which is an unpacking of the Apostles' Creed as the central confession around which Christians can gather.

85.   See http://www.eauk.org/connect/about-us/basis-of-faith.cfm (last visited 7 June 2017).

86.   See http://www.elim.org.uk/Articles/417857/Our_Beliefs.aspx (last visited 7 June 2017).

87.   See http://www.baptist.org.uk/Groups/220595/Declaration_ of_Principle.aspx (last visited 7 June 2017).

88.   See http://www.reformed.org/documents/wlc_w_proofs/ (last visited 7 June 2017).

89.   Karl Barth, *The Heidelberg Catechism for Today* (Richmond: John Knox Press, 1964).

90.   P. Melanchthon, *The Apology of the Augsburg Confession* (Tredition Gmbh, 2011).

91.   For other reformed confessions that might be of interest, see J. T. Dennison, (ed.), *Reformed Confessions of the 16th and 17th Centuries in English Translation: 1523–1552* (Vol. 1; Reformation Heritage Books, 2008).

92.   For an excellent introduction to these see E. J. Bicknell, *A Theological Introduction to the Thirty-nine Articles of the Church of England* (Wipf and Stock Publishers, 2008).

93.   The Apostles' Creed, though not written by the Apostles, is the oldest creed of the Christian church and is the basis for others that followed.

94.   Other than the Apostles' Creed, the Nicene Creed is likely the most universally accepted and recognized statement of the Christian faith. The Nicene Creed was first adopted in AD 325 at the Council of Nicea. The Roman Emperor Constantine convened the Council of Nicea in an attempt to unify the Christian church with one doctrine, especially on the issues of the Trinity and the deity and humanity of Jesus Christ.

95.   The Chalcedonian Creed was adopted at the Council of Chalcedon in AD 451 in Asia Minor as a response to certain heretical views concerning the nature of Christ. This Council of Chalcedon is the fourth of the seven ecumenical councils accepted by Eastern Orthodox, Catholic, and many Protestant Christian churches.

96.   See John 17:21–23.

97.   G. Carey, "The Nature of Ecumenical Vision: Sermon in Luxemburg Cathedral", *One in Christ,* Vol. 34 (1998) pp. 193–194, as quoted in Atherstone and Goddard, *Good Disagreement?,* pp. 128–129.

98.   In the Lambeth Conference of 1888, a fourfold platform for Christian unity was recommended which included the Nicene Creed. The other three parts of the recommendation were: (1) The Old and New Testaments as the final rule and standard of faith; (2) The sacraments of baptism and the Lord's Supper; (3) A locally adapted acceptance of the historic episcopate. Yet the reality is that

in this model, Roman Catholics would find it hard not to include the traditional teaching of the Church in (1) at least to some part; those who do not practise any sacraments (such as adherents of the Salvation Army) would struggle with (2); and non-conformists and non-Episcopalians would struggle with (3)! That leaves a creedal confession, such as the Nicene Creed, as the only expression of unity around which Christians from the widest possible circle could unite without abandoning their own sense of conviction. For further information on some of the thinking that shaped the Lambeth Conference recommendation of 1888 (sometimes called the Chicago–Lambeth Quadrilateral), see W. R. Huntington, *The Church Idea: An Essay Towards Unity* (E. P. Dutton, 1884).

99.   For this version of the Apostles' Creed see http://anglicansonline. org/basics/apostles.html (last visited 7 June 2017). The phrase "he descended into hell" is not part of the earliest expressions of the Apostles' Creed.

100. For this version of the Nicene Creed see http://anglicansonline. org/basics/nicene.html (last visited 7 June 2017).

101. For this version of the Chalcedonian Declaration see http:// anglicansonline.org/basics/chalcedon.html (last visited 7 June 2017).

Toward a Code of Conduct

102. See 1 Corinthians 13:3.

103. Tim Keller and Kathy Keller, T*he Meaning of Marriage: Facing the Complexities of Commitment with the Wisdom of God* (Hodder and Stoughton, 2013), pp. 134ff and the chapter entitled "Loving the Stranger".

104. I unpack this idea further in *The Foundations*, pp. 34ff.

105. For more information on local church covenants see "Local Ecumenical Partnerships: Local Covenants" Churches Together in England, available at http://www.cte.org.uk/Groups/234955/ Home/Resources/Local_Ecumenical_Partnerships/Covenanted_ Partnerships/Local_Covenants_as/Local_Covenants_as.aspx (last visited 7 June 2017).

106. See my comments in the previous chapter on the dialogue between the Roman Catholic Church and the Lutheran Church on the nature of justification and the relationship between grace and works.

107. A helpful reflection on the misunderstandings of ecumenism by Evangelicals, as well as the challenges of ecumenism that still present challenges is I. Randall, "Evangelicals, Ecumenism and Unity: A Case Study of the Evangelical Alliance", *Evangel* 22.3, Autumn 2004.

108. I set out some of the challenges of working together in an earlier book. See Malcolm Duncan, *Kingdom Come: the Local Church as a Catalyst for Social Change* (Oxford: Monarch, 2007), pp. 295ff.

109. To be a formal Local Ecumenical Partnership within the structures of Churches Together in England, a written agreement is required affecting the ministry, congregational life, buildings, and/or mission projects of more than one denomination. This called the Local Ecumenical Partnership Covenant and Constitution. In Churches Together in England there are six forms of ecumenical partnership. They are: (1) Single Congregational Partnerships, where ministry is shared by an Ecumenical Ministry Team and congregations are made up of members with differing denominational affiliation; (2) Congregations in Covenanted Partnership, where there is substantial sharing in worship, church life, mission, and ministry between congregations of differing traditions. Some denominations within the LEP may share ministry and sacraments while others do not; (3) Shared Building Partnerships, where the church building is shared by two or more denominations. Formal agreements come under the Sharing of Church Buildings Act 1969, but there are many instances of informal sharing; (4) Chaplaincy Partnerships, where the chaplains working in an institution commit themselves to work together as an ecumenical team, e.g. in education (universities, joint schools), in prisons, or in hospitals; (5) Mission Partnerships, which include a variety of contexts, e.g. industrial mission, social responsibility, broadcasting, overseas twinning, and others; (6) Education Partnerships, which include Lay Training, Ministerial Training, and joint or shared schools.

110. For more information and guidance on these first five points, please see "Local Ecumenical Partnerships: Guide for Local Churches

to Make an Ecumenical Vision Statement", Churches Together in England, available at http://www.cte.org.uk/Groups/237728/Home/Resources/Local_Ecumenical_Partnerships/Writing_an_Ecumenical/Writing_an_Ecumenical.aspx (last visited 7 June 2017).

111. See "Churches Together in Hitchin", available at http://www.cthitchin.org.uk/ (last visited 7 June 2017).

112. See *The Foundations*, pp. 215ff, for some examples.

113. See "Gather", available at http://www.gather.global/ for further information (last visited 7 June 2017).

114. See http://www.gather.global/project/christ-first-middlesbrough/ as an example of what Christ First do (last visited 14 June 2017).

115. See "Bath Churches Together and Bath Christian Action Network", available at http://www.bathchurches.org.uk/welcome.htm (last visited 7 June 2017).

116. See "Gweini: Serving the Christian Voluntary Sector in Wales", available at http://www.gweini.org.uk (last visited 7 June 2017).

117. See "ARC: Association of Related Churches Ireland", available at http://arcireland.org (last visited 7 June 2017).

118. As articulated in the previous chapter, I suggest either the Apostles' Creed, the Nicene Creed or the Chalcedonian Declaration.

119. For a powerful example of this, see my discussion of the schism in the evangelical world that was represented by the disagreement between Martyn Lloyd-Jones and John Stott in *The Foundations*, pp. 25ff. Steve Clifford has also offered some helpful reflections on this issue. See Steve Clifford, *One: Unity in Diversity, A Personal Journey* (Oxford: Monarch, 2017) pp. 189ff.

120. See J. T. Flynn, "Evangelical Truth: A Personal Plea for Unity, Integrity, and Faithfulness – John Stott", *Religious Studies Review*, 32(3) (2006), pp. 178–79.

Liberty not Licence

121. See Romans 14–15, for example, and 1 Corinthians 14.

122. See Galatians 3:26–29.

123. See Galatians 2–4.

124. Paul wrote to "all God's beloved in Rome" (Romans 1:7); he described the Galatians as "friends" (Galatians 4:12, 28); he wrote to the "saints who are in Ephesus" (Ephesians 1:1); he began his letter to the Philippians, "Paul and Timothy, servants of Christ Jesus, To all the saints in Christ Jesus who are in Philippi, together with the bishops and the deacons" (Philippians 1:1), among other examples.

125. That is not to say he was reticent to challenge. Remember he told the church in Corinth to put the man caught in sexual sin out of the worshipping community so that restoration could take place (see 1 Corinthians 5), and, as highlighted earlier, he was quite open to using strong language to challenge those who were bringing error into the early church.

126. See Philippians 1:27–28, for example: "Only, live your life in a manner worthy of the gospel of Christ, so that, whether I come and see you or am absent and hear about you, I will know that you are standing firm in one spirit, striving side by side with one mind for the faith of the gospel, and are in no way intimidated by your opponents. For them this is evidence of their destruction, but of your salvation. And this is God's doing."

127. See Colossians 3; 1 Thessalonians 4 and Paul's epistle to Philemon for examples of him reminding his listeners/readers that they were united by Christ and not by culture, status, or any other characteristic.

128. See Philippians 2:1–5 in particular: "If then there is any encouragement in Christ, any consolation from love, any sharing in the Spirit, any compassion and sympathy, make my joy complete: be of the same mind, having the same love, being in full accord and of one mind. Do nothing from selfish ambition or conceit, but in humility regard others as better than yourselves. Let each of you look not to your own interests, but to the interests of others. Let the same mind be in you that was in Christ Jesus."

129. I refer you to Tom Wright's contribution to Atherstone and Goddard, *Good Disagreement?* for a fuller unpacking of some of the themes contained in this chapter: "Pastoral Theology for Perplexing Topics: Paul and *Adiaphora*", pp. 63ff.

130. See *The Foundations*, pp. 98ff for a key conversation around this.

131. The whole letter to the Corinthians could be seen as an exploration of unity, but of particular interest to us here is 1 Corinthians 14 which can only be read in the light of the messages laced throughout the rest of the epistle. Romans 14 and 15 are invaluable for helping us understand how to journey through the issues of primary and secondary significance today. Both passages deal with similar types of issues

132. See Wright, "Pastoral Theology for Perplexing Topics", p. 64.

133. See *The Foundations,* pp. 98ff, for my engagement with this issue in more detail.

134. See the pivotal chapter: Romans 12.

135. See Ephesians 4, Colossians 3, Philippians 3:17–19 and 1 Thessalonians 4, for example.

136. For a helpful reflection on the some of the issues around the principle of disputable matters see Martin Davie, "Why Issues of Human Sexuality Are Not Adiaphora": a paper presented to the Church of England Evangelical Council at a residential meeting in January 2016. Available at http://www.ceec.info/uploads/4/4/2/7/44274161/why_issues_of_human_sexuality_are_not_adiaphora_-_m_davie.pdf (last visited 8 June 2017).

137. See Wright, "Pastoral Theology for Perplexing Topics", p.70.

138. See Wright, "Pastoral Theology for Perplexing Topics", p.76.

139. See Tom Wright's comments on Romans 14:21–23 in Tom Wright, *Paul for Everyone, Romans Part 2* (London: SPCK, 2004), pp. 108–109.

140. Calvin sets out some of his arguments for Christian liberty in the nineteenth chapter of his third book in his *Institutes*. The chapter is entitled "On Christian Liberty", and in it he sets out three divisions

concerning Christian unity: (1) The essential nature of Christian doctrine; (2) The importance of remembering "the weak" (in his original he highlights the failure of those, such as Epicureans, who disregard the conscience of the weak); (3) The issue of offence and how it is given or received. See H. Beveridge (trans.), *The Institutes of Christian Religion by John Calvin* (Grand Rapids: Eerdmans, 1989). *Book Third – Continued: The Mode of Obtaining the Grace of Christ. The Benefits It Confers and the Effects Resulting From It*, pp. 130ff.

141. See Davie, "Why Issues of Human Sexuality Are Not Adiaphora", p. 6.

142. Consider these comments from Luther in his work *The Freedom of a Christian*. See Martin Luther, *The Freedom of a Christian* (Philadelphia: Fortress Press, 2008):

... hear of this freedom of faith, immediately turn it into an occasion for the flesh and think that now all things are allowed them. They want to show that they are free men and Christians only by despising and finding fault with ceremonies, traditions and human laws; as if they were Christians because on stated days they do not fast or eat meat when others fast, or because they do not use the accustomed prayers, and with upturned nose scoff at the precepts of men, although they utterly disregard all else that pertains to the Christian religion. The extreme opposite of these are those who rely for their salvation solely on the reverent observance of ceremonies, as if they would be saved because on certain days they fast or abstain from meats, or pray certain prayers; these make a boast of the precepts of the church and of the fathers, and do not care a fig for the things which are of the essence of our faith. Plainly, both are in error because they neglect the weightier things which are necessary for salvation, and quarrel so noisily about trifling and unnecessary matters... How much better is the teaching of St. Paul... who bids us to take a middle course and condemns both sides when he says "Let not him who eats despise him who abstains, and let not him who abstains pass judgement on him who eats" [Rom 14:3]. Here you see that they who neglect and disparage ceremonies, not out of piety, but out of mere contempt, are reproved since the Apostle teaches us not to despise them. Such men are puffed up by knowledge. On the other hand, he teaches those who insist on the ceremonies not to judge the others, for neither party acts towards the other according to the love that edifies. Wherefore we ought to listen to Scripture which teaches that we should not go aside to the right or to the left [Deut 28:14] but follow the statutes of the law which are right, "rejoicing the heart" [Ps.19:8]. As a man is not righteous because he keeps and clings to the works and forms of the ceremonies, so also will a man not be counted righteous because he neglects and despises them. (pp. 310–11)

143. Wright, "Pastoral Theology for Perplexing Topics", p. 81.

144. See Wright, "Pastoral Theology for Perplexing Topics", p.78, particularly the following: "But – and we should note this once again – Paul does not apply this [adiaphora] to questions of sexual ethics (or for that matter to extortion, murder, violence, lying, mutual lawsuits, and so forth.)"

145. See The Foundations, pp. 98ff.

Core Principles – Three Commitments for Unity

146. Throughout The Implications I have used language that is rooted in the conviction that our unity is not something we create or strive for, but rather something that we have been given by God through Christ. We do not make it; we preserve and protect it. This is the core foundation of One for All: The Foundations upon which the implications of our unity are built.

147. See Luke 8:26–39. Some versions of the story describe the region as the region of the Gadaranes and others the region of the Gergesenes.

148. See verse 27.

149. See verse 35.

150. Essentially, I believe that divorce is permissible in certain situations and that remarriage is possible, but that each situation must be addressed individually and sensitively.

151. Jean Vanier, Our Life Together: A Memoir in Letters (London: Darton, Longman and Todd, 2008), pp. 296–297.

152. Eugene Peterson, *The Word Made Flesh: The Language of Jesus in His Stories and Prayers* (London: Hodder and Stoughton, 2008), p. 44. In the first half of the book, Peterson unpacks the journey of Jesus with His disciples through the "enemy" territory of Samaria and reflects on the remarkable personal way in which Jesus addresses them and exposes their prejudices, their fears, and their hopes. He also helps us to see the way in which relationship sits at the heart of true ministry.

153. See "From Castles to Conversations: Reflections on How to Disagree Well" by Lis Goddard and Clare Hendy, a discussion on their differing views on the role of women in the church, in Atherstone and Goddard, *Good Disagreement?*, pp. 151ff. This method of communication and learning is intriguingly different to the more traditional didactic model of presentation.

154. In *The Foundations* I reflect on the example of the some of the early Church Fathers in putting a higher emphasis on remaining united than they did on other theological issues. See pp. 44ff.

155. See John 13:27.

156. See Mark 10:35–40, when James and John wanted to be promoted to places of great honour with Christ, presumably at the expense of the other disciples. In addition, see Luke 9:51–56, when James and John wanted to call fire down from heaven. In both cases, Jesus refused their requests without breaking His relationship with them.

157. See Matthew 16:21–23, when Jesus rebuked Peter for his refusal to accept that Christ will suffer.

158. See Romans 5:6–11.

159. See 1 John 4:18–21.

160. See Hebrews 13:5.

161. See Hebrews 7:25.

One for Purpose

162. The glorious purpose of our unity is set out in the prayer of the Lord Jesus in John 17 which I exegete in *The Foundations*, pp. 84ff.

163. See the powerful images of Psalm 133. This idea of the visible manifestation of unity is unpacked in *The Foundations*, pp. 228ff under the title "The Blessing of Unity".

164. See P. Ward, *Growing Up Evangelical: Youthwork and the Making of a Subculture* (Wipf and Stock Publishers, 2013).

165. See "Gen Z: Rethinking Culture", a resource produced by British Youth for Christ and available at https://yfc.uk/product/gen-z/ (last visited 8 June 2017).

166. See https://www.youthscape.co.uk/research/publications/losing-heart to download the report (last visited 8 June 2017).

167. James Emery White, "Meet Generation Z", available at http://www.crosswalk.com/blogs/dr-james-emery-white/meet-generation-z.html (last visited 8 June 2017).

168. Matthew 16:18.

169. For a powerful exploration of this see Mark Griffiths, *One Generation from Extinction: How the Church Connects with the Unchurched Child* (Oxford: Monarch Books, 2009).

170. See Psalm 145:4.

171. See Habakkuk 2:14.

172. See Revelation 7:9.

Malcolm would love to hear your thoughts or stories of unity and invites you to connect with this subject on the Facebook Page "One for All" which can be found by searching @unitedforapurpose. He's keen to hear stories of what happens when churches work together and some of the challenges that this presents us with. He'd also love to learn from your stories and thoughts on unity.

Malcolm blogs at www.malcolmduncan.typepad. com, can be followed on Facebook at RevMalcolmDuncan, on twitter at @MalcolmJDuncan and can be contacted at malcolm.duncan@goldhill.org He'd love to connect with you

One for All

The Foundations

The importance of unity in a fractured world

"A tour de force in the call to a new unity. Each generation needs to grapple with this quest and Malcolm has met this challenge afresh."

Lyndon Bowring, Executive Chairman of CARE

HOW UNITED IS THE CHURCH IN THE WORLD TODAY?

Scars of division and suspicion continue to mark us – we have accepted them as inevitable and unavoidable. *One For All* is a timely and prophetic call to the church to be faithful to God's Word and devoted to Jesus Christ so that His vision, recorded in John 17, the prayer in which He called us to be one as He and the Father are one so that the world might know, can be revealed through us in our time.

"A wonderful and insightful look at the clear biblical mandate for unity. I found myself captivated by the wisdom pouring from each page. Get it today and be inspired to play your part."

Gavin Calver, Director of Mission, Evangelical Alliance; Chair of Spring Harvest Planning Group

978-0-85721-810-0 | 978-0-85721-811-7

www.lionhudson.com